HISTORY'S MOST EPIC FAILS!

wren & rook

ATHENA KUGBLENU
ILLUSTRATED BY NICOLE MILES

First published in Great Britain in 2025 by Wren & Rook

ISBN: 978 1 5263 6682 5

SRD

MIX
Paper | Supporting
responsible forestry
FSC™ C104740

Wren & Rook
An imprint of
Hachette Children's Group
Part of Hodder & Stoughton Limited
Carmelite House
50 Victoria Embankment
London EC4Y 0DZ

An Hachette UK Company
www.hachette.co.uk
www.hachettechildrens.co.uk

Printed and bound in India by Manipal Technologies Limited, Manipal

FOR RADHA 'PSYCHE' BEDESSEE

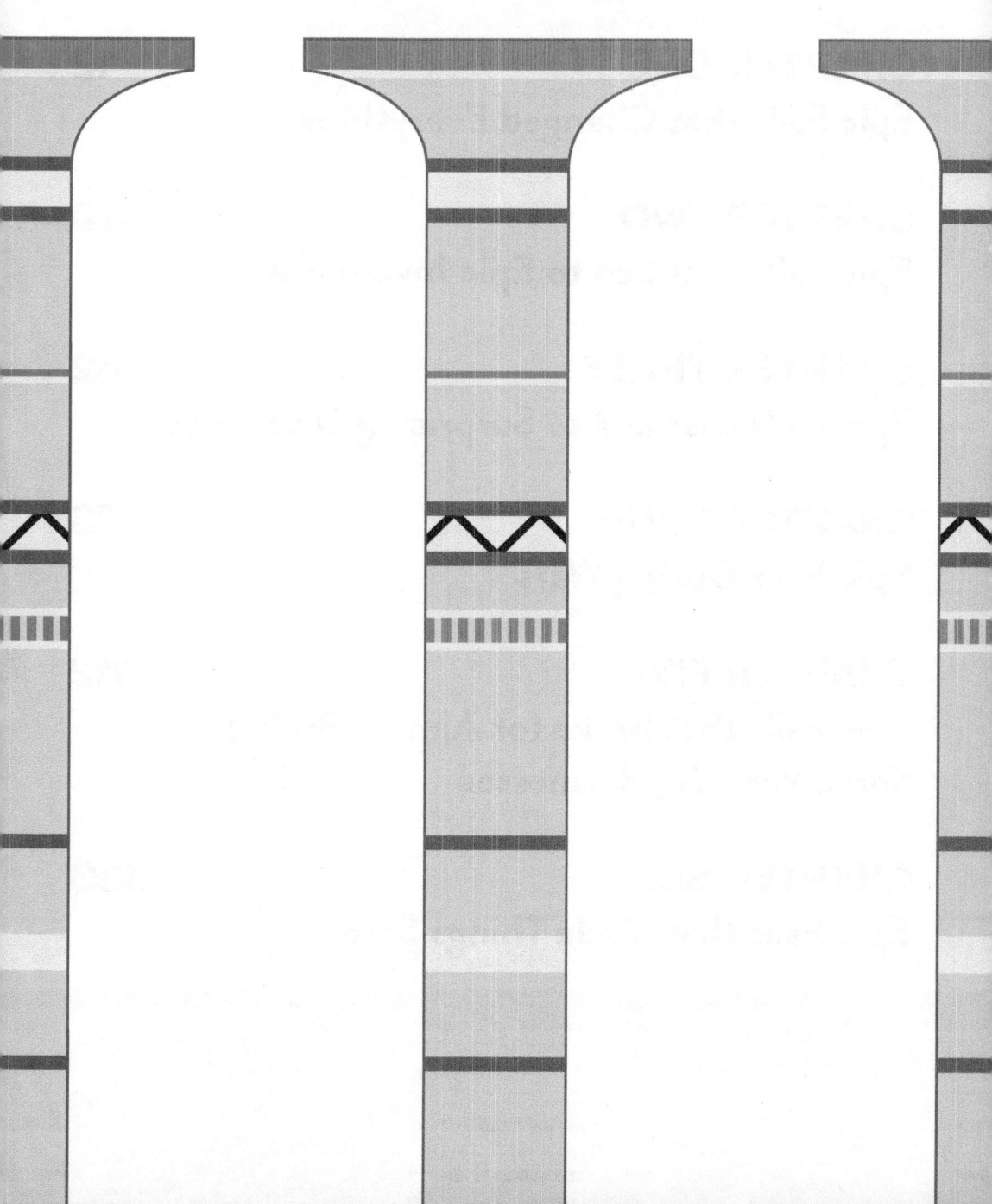

CONTENTS

INTRODUCTION

Some people are afraid of spiders. Some are afraid of heights. I am scared of something that's slightly harder to explain. I have a fear of . . . **FAILURE!**

Whenever I have to do something new, or something I don't think I am very good at, the same questions pop into my head:

WHAT IF I LOOK SILLY?

WHAT IF I GET IT WRONG?

WHAT IF SOMETHING BAD HAPPENS?

But having a fear of failure makes no sense because **EVERYBODY, EVERYWHERE HAS FAILED AT SOMETHING**. Babies fail again and again before they learn to walk. Kids fail when they are learning to tie up their shoelaces. Adults fail too. Have you ever watched a grown-up try to build flat-pack furniture? It doesn't always go to plan! But failure is actually useful, **BECAUSE WE CAN LEARN FROM OUR MISTAKES!**

And it's not just **OUR** mistakes that we learn from, either. History is full of **EPIC FAILS** from other people that can teach us something, too. Some of those failures were little ones. Some failures were absolutely **MASSIVE** and had ginormous consequences. Consequences so big they taught us not to make the same mistakes again.

Fails come in all shapes and sizes. Because there are so many failures throughout history, with so many different results, we've got a handy way to help you make sense of them all. Introducing the **FAIL-TASTIC . . .**

... FAIL-O-METER!

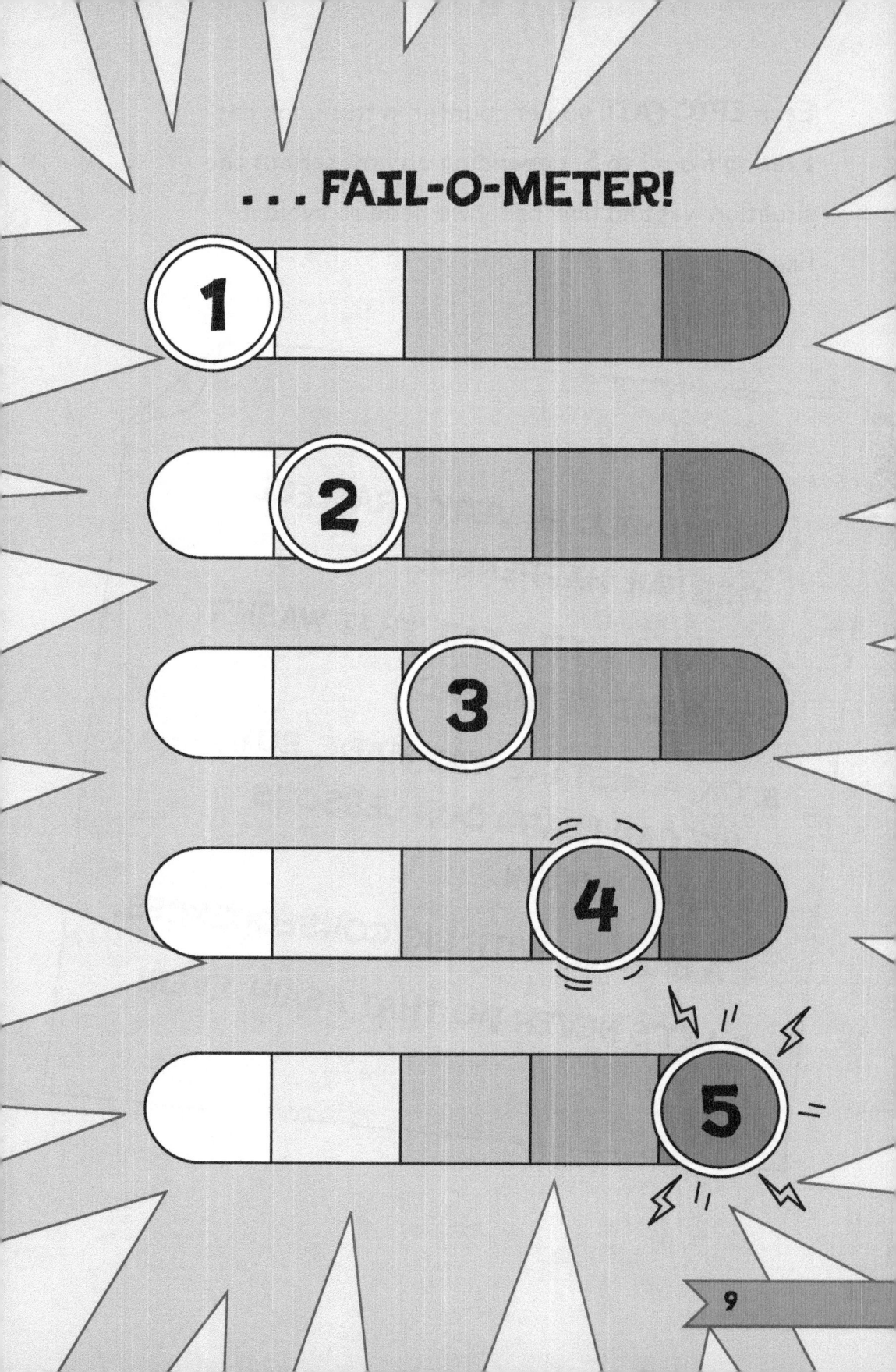

Each **EPIC FAIL** you encounter in this book has a rating from 1 to 5, depending on how serious the situation was and how badly we need to avoid it happening again:

1. WE SHOULD BE VERY GRATEFUL THIS FAIL HAPPENED!

2. PHEW! A LITTLE FAIL THAT WASN'T TOO BAD IN THE END.

3. OK, A MISTAKE WAS MADE. BUT WE CAN LEARN OUR LESSONS AND MOVE ON.

4. A BIG FAIL, WITH BIG CONSEQUENCES.

5. LET'S NEVER DO THAT AGAIN. EVER!

So, get ready to learn about some epic mess-ups. Some will inspire you to believe in yourself and keep trying. Some will have you gasping at the past and wondering what lessons we can learn to make sure those mistakes are never made again. And some will even have you believing in good luck.

After reading this book, you'll have found out about so many epic historical mishaps that you'll spot fails everywhere. Fails are part of our past, part of our present and part of our future. They are not to be feared at all. The only thing we should be afraid of is **NOT LEARNING** from them!

CHAPTER
ONE

EPIC FAILS
THAT CHANGED
EVERYTHING

Many famous events in history happened because of an **EPIC FAIL**. Some of these fails would have seemed pretty small at the time, like forgetting a bit of kit or not locking a door. But some of these tiny fails had impacts so big we still talk about them today.

There are also many famous stories from history that resulted from **EPIC FAILS** that we've completely forgotten about. These stories are so remarkable we simply must remember them here. They are a great reminder of how useful it is to know the **FULL** story behind a **MOMENTOUS** event.

The one thing all these fails have in common is that they resulted in something really legendary, disastrous or outrageous, and they **CHANGED EVERYTHING**.

THE FAIL: A GATE WAS LEFT UNLOCKED

WHEN: 1453

WHERE: CONSTANTINOPLE (NOW KNOWN AS ISTANBUL)

WHAT HAPPENED? CONTROL OF A SUPER-MEGACITY WAS WON BY THE OTTOMAN EMPIRE

Constantinople – which is now known as Istanbul – was founded way back in 330 CE, by Roman Emperor Constantine. It was the heart of the Byzantine Empire – sometimes called the Eastern Roman Empire – and has remained a booming place of **TRADE** and commerce for over 1,000 years.

Because it was such a such an **IMPORTANT** city, it faced constant attacks from other people who wanted to have it for themselves. It was bit like a must-have toy – throw one into a room full of kids and they will all fight for it!

In 408 CE, Emperor Theodosius II built a **MASSIVE** wall to keep pesky intruders out. And it worked! For centuries, nobody could successfully attack the city and take it over.

But in 1453, a man called Sultan Mehmed II thought he'd have a go. He was the leader of the Ottoman Empire and had **BIG** ambitions. Plus, he had a secret weapon: gunpowder. The wall was built well before gunpowder was invented and wasn't designed to cope with weapons that used it. Maybe, just maybe, his big guns would be able to knock it down . . .

Mehmed II attacked Constantinople with the most advanced cannons of the day.

The biggest were 8 meters long and fired cannonballs that weighed 600 kg. That's as heavy as a **GRAND PIANO**. Imagine someone chucking a grand piano at your front door! (Couldn't they just ring the bell?)

After a massive siege, Mehmed launched one final attack. You can imagine Mehmed's troops charging the wall, expecting to tear it down . . . only to find they were able to stroll in, climb to the top of the wall and raise the Ottoman flag. Why was the wall so easy to get past? One source suggests that a gate was left open, and that open gate let Mehmed and the Ottomans take over the city. What an **EPIC FAIL**!

Constantinople would probably still have fallen if the gate was locked. Remember – the wall was never built to withstand powerful weapons. But it was certainly made a lot easier because someone left the gate unlocked!

RATING:

4

The fall of Constantinople changed everything. It signalled the end of the Byzantine Empire, which had been powerful for many years. Lots of very smart people ran away from the city and ended up in Italy. Some historians think this was a spark for the Renaissance – a time of great innovation and invention that took hold in the Italian city states of Florence, Venice, Bologna and Rome.

THE FAIL: A LIBRARY GOT BURNED DOWN BY ACCIDENT

WHEN: 48 BCE

WHERE: ALEXANDRIA, IN ANCIENT EGYPT

WHAT HAPPENED? LOTS OF AMAZING KNOWLEDGE WAS DESTROYED FOREVER. OOOPS

The Great Library of Alexandria was one of the largest libraries in the world. In those days, people didn't have books – they had scrolls, which are long sheets of paper that you have to roll up. Some people think it may have had 400,000. Whichever number is right, the library contained a lot of knowledge!

The Great Library of Alexandria became known as a place for intellectuals and thinkers (like us, at Epic History Towers!).

It was a hugely important place in the Egyptian Empire.

Until Julius Caesar burned it down by accident. Definitely a **BIG** 'whooopsie!'

In 48 BCE there was a civil war in Egypt between Cleopatra and her little brother Ptolemy XIII. A civil war is when people who are from the same country or empire fight each other. Julius Caesar quite liked Cleopatra and decided he would get involved and give her a helping hand.

At one point, Caesar was trapped in the port of Alexandria. He thought setting fire to pesky enemy ships around him would create a path for him to flee. That sounds like a good idea on paper (or on a scroll!) but in practice it's not, because fires spread! Especially when buildings are mostly made from wood and are stuffed full of paper. Predictably, the fires got out of control and reached the famous library. An absolutely **EPIC FAIL**!

Over time, people told different stories about the fire fail depending on whether they liked Caesar or not. If you liked him, you told people that he just burned down a little bit of it. If you hated him, you told people that he burned down the whole thing. Either way, it is still an **EPIC FAIL** because it was **DEFINITELY** burned and many secrets of the Egyptian Empire remain unknown because of all the scrolls that were lost.

RATING:

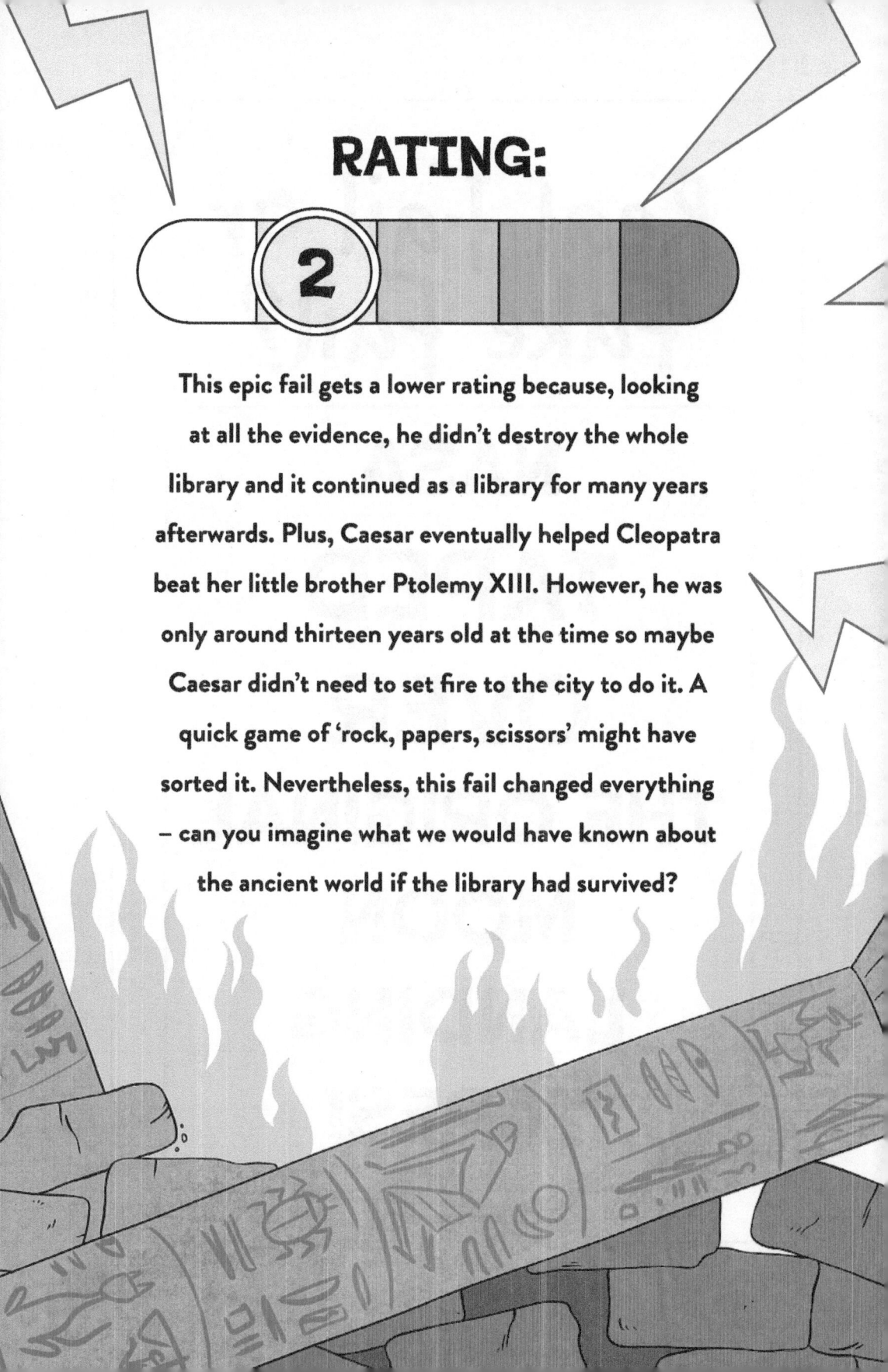

2

This epic fail gets a lower rating because, looking at all the evidence, he didn't destroy the whole library and it continued as a library for many years afterwards. Plus, Caesar eventually helped Cleopatra beat her little brother Ptolemy XIII. However, he was only around thirteen years old at the time so maybe Caesar didn't need to set fire to the city to do it. A quick game of 'rock, papers, scissors' might have sorted it. Nevertheless, this fail changed everything – can you imagine what we would have known about the ancient world if the library had survived?

Real Fail or Fake Fail?

NASA TAPED OVER THE ORIGINAL MOON LANDING TAPES!

Find the answer on page 236.

THE FAIL: A MAP-MAKER THOUGHT AMERIGO VESPUCCI DISCOVERED AMERICA

WHEN: 1507

WHERE: GERMANY

WHAT HAPPENED? THEY GAVE THE AMERICAS A NAME THAT STUCK!

Let's start with a fun fact: 'America' is the only continent on Earth named after a real person and it is all because of an **EPIC FAIL**.

In 1507 a cartographer – someone who makes maps for a job – made a map. His name was **MARTIN WALDSEEMÜLLER**, he was German and he was the first European to make a map that showed America as a whole, separate continent. You should definitely find this map. It looks very much like the maps we are familiar with today. This was a **SPECTACULAR** achievement for someone with no tools like a smartphone or the internet. The problem was, there was one **BIG** mistake on it. He guessed that the new continent he had drawn was called '**AMERICA**'.

Christopher Columbus had been to the Americas on a voyage of discovery and, ultimately, exploitation of this 'new' land. But a sailor named Amerigo Vespucci sailed across the ocean, too. For some reason, Waldseemüller thought Amerigo did it before Columbus, and he mistakenly added his name to the map.

EPIC FAIL ALERT!

He made 1,000 copies of this map with the wrong name. The map was passed from person to person and the name 'America' was shared far and wide. Waldseemüller soon realised his mistake and made more maps without the name 'America' written on them. But it was too late – 'America' stuck.

Imagine if he hadn't made this **EPIC FAIL**! America would be called the United States of Chistopherland! Or Columbusworld! Oh wait, maybe they would have stuck with Columbia – which is how the country Columbia got its name!

NAMES AREN'T MY DEPARTMENT!

Amerigo Vespucci never learned that the continents he visited would be named after him, as the maps didn't reach Spain, where he lived, until after he died. However, I think he would be chuffed that his name is now probably one of the most famous names in the world. He even has my favourite kind of coffee named after him – the americano!

RATING:

This fail CHANGED EVERYTHING, as America is the name given to two continents (North America and South America). However, whether the countries were named after Amerigo Vespucci or Columbus, both names represent Europeans travelling to countries where Indigenous people were already living, and taking those countries over for themselves – otherwise known as exploitation and colonialism.

THE FAIL: LOTS OF CHINESE SHIPS WERE DESTROYED

WHEN: 1500S

WHERE: CHINA

WHAT HAPPENED? THE EUROPEANS STARTED SAILING MORE AND WERE ABLE TO PICK UP WHERE THEY LEFT OFF!

In the 1400s and 1500s, Chinese shipbuilders were the best in the world. At one point, they had over 3,500 ships sailing about. Boats were good for merchants and sailors, but the leaders on dry land in China didn't care much for them. The emperor at the time, Emperor Hongxi, thought ships were too expensive and not that impressive.

In 1433, China decided to stop all this sailing malarky once and for all. They ordered their existing ships to be destroyed and stopped building new ones altogether. Some historians think it was an **EPIC FAIL** to abandon sailing, because once they did, Chinese influence on the rest of the world decreased. Just a few decades later, European countries decided to sail around the world and made a lot of money for themselves, using technology that was nowhere near as advanced as what existed in China at the time. Western Europe set themselves up for centuries of power that still impacts many parts of the world today.

RATING:

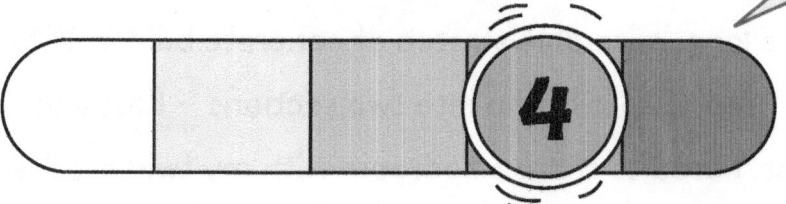

It scores very highly because this decision really did **CHANGE EVERYTHING.** Now, when we think of the Age of Exploration, the great Chinese ships don't spring to mind – we think of European ones that were tiny in comparison. But maybe if they had kept sailing, China would not have built the Great Wall of China and become the country it is today?

THE FAIL: TELLING PEOPLE A CHECKPOINT WAS BEING OPENED, WHEN IT WASN'T

WHEN: 1989

WHERE: GERMANY

WHAT HAPPENED? PEOPLE CROSSED THE BERLIN WALL BEFORE IT WAS TAKEN DOWN

You might have heard of the **BERLIN WALL** already. It was a long, miserable stretch of concrete built in 1961 and used to split Berlin into two sections – East and West. I used to share a bedroom with my twin brother and we would divide our room using stuffed toys. It was a bit like that, but much more serious.

It was very difficult for Germans to live in a divided country. They weren't allowed to cross the border and it meant some people were separated from loved ones. A lot of people wanted the wall to go.

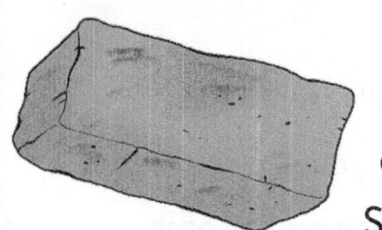

On 9 November 1989, a man on the east side of the wall, called Günter Schabowski, told the world in a press conference that people would be able to cross the border 'immediately'. Germans were delighted. They raced to the checkpoint in the wall so they could cross it as soon as possible.

Only . . . this was an **EPIC FAIL** from Schabowski! People were going to be allowed to apply to cross the border, not just cross it willy-nilly.

The Berlin Wall still formed part of a border. To cross borders you need to do things like show someone important your **ID**. However, the people didn't care about this. They had been told they were allowed to cross **ON THE NEWS**! Surely if it was on the news, it must be true? Eventually, there were too many people trying to cross at the checkpoint to turn away, and everyone was allowed to pass.

The resulting scenes from the evening of 9 November 1989 are now world famous. People can be seen hugging, dancing and even handing each other flowers. Eventually, someone had the brilliant idea to scale the wall, and you can see pictures of jubilant Germans trying to dance on top of it without falling off. Which is not an easy thing to do – so please don't try it yourself!

RATING:

1

If anything, this was a **GOOD EPIC FAIL**. It gave power to the people. Nobody in charge saw the point in stopping them because the wall was coming down anyway. Thanks to Schabowski, it happened a whole lot faster Sometimes all you need is an **EPIC FAIL** to show the grown-ups in charge how to really get something done fast.

THE FAIL: THINKING THAT HIS BFF, CLEOPATRA, HAD DIED!

WHEN: 31 BCE

WHERE: ALEXANDRIA

WHAT HAPPENED? ROME GOT ITS FIRST EMPEROR!

Cleopatra was the last queen of ancient Egypt. In 31 BCE she faced her final fight against the Romans: the **EPIC** Battle of Actium.

On one side was Octavian, Julius Caesar's great-nephew and his chosen heir. On the other was Mark Antony, Caesar's general, who wanted the job too. In between was Cleopatra, who had a son with Julius Caesar and was in a relationship with Mark Antony at the time of the battle. Oh, did I mention she had twins with Mark Antony as well? Understandably, Cleopatra chose Mark Antony's side. If that all sounds very complicated, that's because it was!

Cleopatra's support of Mark Antony made everyone in Rome very nervous – maybe she was using him to expand her Egyptian Empire into Rome? Could Mark Antony be convinced to give Rome to his lady friend?

The tension got too much! Rather than wait for Cleopatra to get her hands on the Roman Empire, Octavian decided to declare war in 31 BCE at Actium, in Greece. A mighty naval battle took place between the two sides. Soon, it became clear that Octavian's ships were better and stronger. Cleopatra ran back to Alexandria, with her faithful Antony not far behind.

Sensing victory, Octavian chased them and won the next battle in Alexandria too. Feeling a bit upset about losing all these battles, Cleopatra decided to hide in a mausoleum – which is a very fancy place where you can bury someone important who has died.

Soon, word got out that Cleopatra was hiding in a mausoleum, but this turned into an **EPIC FAIL**.

The news spread, and by the time Mark Antony was told where she was, people mistakenly thought she had died!

Heartbroken, and fearing he would not be able to live without his beloved Cleopatra, Mark Antony decided to take his own life. While he was dying, he was told that Cleopatra was, in fact, alive. **WOO HOO!** Well, not really 'woo hoo', because it was too late to remove his sword from his stomach. But he was able to send a message to her as his last act. He made two requests. He wanted Cleopatra to stop fighting and to be friends with Octavian.

The news of Mark Antony's death and his message reached Cleopatra. Sadly, she wasn't that impressed with either piece of information.

She was about to lose her Egyptian Empire and wasn't in the mood to face being friends with Octavian or living without Mark Antony. Tragically, she took her own life too.

With both his enemies now dead, Octavian renamed himself Augustus, took Egypt for himself and became the first leader of the Roman Empire. That sounds like a **FAIL** that resulted in a mighty big change to me!

RATING:

This gets a low score, considering the very grave consequences, because Mark Antony and Cleopatra were already losing against Octavian. They just made his victory a little bit easier.

THE FAIL: HENRY VIII WAS OBSESSED WITH HAVING A MALE HEIR!

WHEN: BETWEEN 1509 AND 1547

WHERE: BRITAIN

WHAT HAPPENED? THE CHURCH OF ENGLAND WAS CREATED!

Henry VIII is one of England's best-known monarchs and he is famous for something he was desperate to do: make male heirs. And **LOTS** of them.

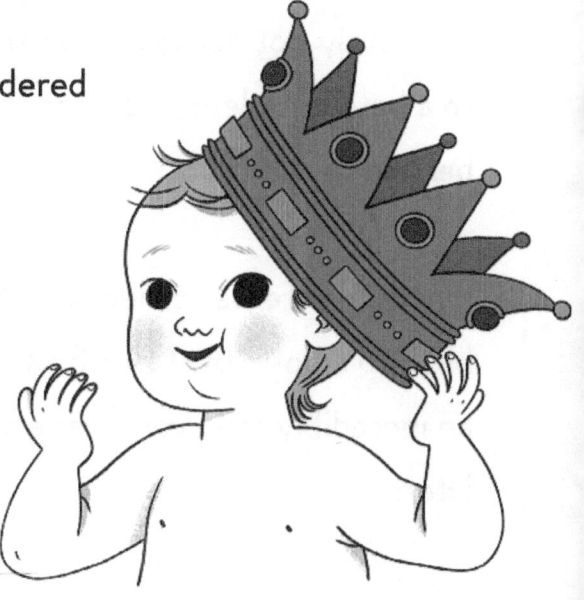

In his day, boys were considered better than girls because people didn't think girls would make good leaders. What a load of nonsense – that sounds like a chapter I should have put in *History's Most Epic Fibs*! But, because people in the 1500s truly believed this, Henry VIII made it his mission to have lots of sons to ensure the Tudor line of monarchs would go on for a long time.

First, he married Katherine of Aragon and she became pregnant with a daughter, Mary. This, of course, was not Katherine's fault – it's not like you can go to the market and pick up a baby boy. Henry didn't see things this way and he divorced her. To do so, he had to invent the Church of England because the leader of the Catholic Church would not let him get divorced.

He then got himself another wife called Anne Boleyn. She had a daughter, named Elizabeth. Again, it was absolutely not her fault that she wasn't able to give birth to a boy, but Henry decided that it was and decided to behead her. **YIKES**.

His third wife was called Jane Seymour, and she did give birth to a boy. **YAY!** But Edward's birth was followed by an incredibly sad event. Jane Seymour died twelve days later.

So, you guessed it, Henry VIII married again because one son wasn't enough. This time it was Anne of Cleves's turn. She wasn't able to have any children with Henry but she did manage to keep her head and escape with a divorce.

The wives kept coming: next up was Catherine Howard. Together, they were not able to have any children. Not only did she not produce a male heir, but Henry was also convinced she was not faithful to him, so she got beheaded too!

You can say lots of things about Henry VIII, but you can definitely say he was persistent. By the time of his last marriage to Katherine Parr in 1543 he was old (well, fifty-two was considered old in those days) and in poor health. Katherine Parr wasn't able to have children with him, but she manged to convince Henry to be grateful for the children he **DID** have. He decided to continue his Tudor legacy by allowing his daughters, Mary and Elizabeth, to be queens. You might know them better as Mary I and Elizabeth I.

RATING:

4

Henry's quest to have a male heir changed the major religion of his country and the Church of England is a huge institution today. The Tudor royal line did stop when Queen Elizabeth I died in 1603, but we haven't stopped talking about him. Maybe he got the Tudor legacy he always wanted after all?

Fails for Thought

Can you imagine what the
world would look like today
if any of these fails hadn't
happened? What might have
turned out differently? These
fails had HUMONGOUS
consequences. Which
ones do you think had
the BIGGEST effect?

CHAPTER TWO

EPIC FAILS THAT LED TO EPIC INVENTIONS

If at first you don't succeed, try and try again. This sounds like good advice but it's much easier said than done! It takes a lot of confidence and patience to keep trying to do something, especially if it doesn't work out first time.

A really good way to feel better about these kinds of failures is to look at all the people who never gave up and went on to create epic **INVENTIONS**. Everywhere in history we can find examples of people who **KEPT GOING** and believed in themselves. Get ready to be inspired by our collection of **EPIC FAILS** from truly epic people!

THE FAIL: THOMAS EDISON WAS TERRIBLE AT SCHOOL AND KEPT INVENTING THINGS THAT DIDN'T WORK!

WHEN: EARLY 1900S

WHERE: UNITED STATES OF AMERICA

WHAT HAPPENED? EDISON ENDED UP BECOMING ONE OF THE MOST WELL-KNOWN INVENTORS IN THE WORLD

Thomas Edison didn't invent the first light bulb (and if you've read *History's Most Epic Fibs*, you'll know all about that!) but he is **WORLD FAMOUS** for inventing the light bulb that we use today.

Even so, he experienced some **EPIC FAILS**.

Firstly, Edison didn't do very well in school. In fact, his school was so rude about his abilities, his mum decided to take him out and teach him at home. His mum encouraged his interests in machinery and building things, and hey presto: an **EPIC FAIL** was overcome!

However, not everything worked out when Edison became an inventor. He had an idea for an electric pen that would make copies of a document. It was like a normal pen but with a needle at the end of it. The idea was that you'd put sheets of paper underneath a sheet of paper you wanted copied, and the needle would pierce through the top sheet, transferring ink to the bottom sheets. It didn't work very well and turned into a very messy and very expensive idea. **BUT** his **EPIC FAIL** turned into an **EPIC SUCCESS** because it caught the eye of another inventor called Samuel O'Reilly.

O'Reilly realised that the pen wasn't very good at copying things, but it was a wonderful way to make marks underneath skin. Don't flinch – it sounds horrible, but it's really not! Edison had invented an early tattoo machine. If Edison hadn't made his **EPIC FAIL**, we might not have the tattoo machine that we use today. Edison was also obsessed with electric cars. He spent lots of time and money trying to build batteries that could make cars move, but he was never successful and cars ended up being reliant on petrol for over a hundred years. Even though it was an **EPIC FAIL** it can **NEVER** be described as a failure! He started a journey that took **DECADES** to complete, and it's only recently the car industry agrees that using petrol isn't the best idea, because one day, petrol is going to run out. We definitely have to appreciate Edison for trying so hard to make an electric car, and we also have to say: 'Thanks, Thomas – you were right all along!'

RATING:

1

All Edison needed was someone to believe in him, and luckily his mum did. He was clearly a creative thinker and there was potential in so many of his ideas, even though he wasn't always right. Edison never gave up and that's why many of his EPIC FAILS became EPIC INVENTIONS!

Real Fail or Fake Fail?

A WORLD-FAMOUS BRITISH ENGINEER MADE A MASSIVE PASSENGER SHIP THAT COULD CARRY 4,000 PEOPLE, BUT HE COULDN'T FIND 4,000 WHO WANTED TO SAIL IN IT!

Find the answer on page 236.

THE FAIL: INVENTOR RICHARD JAMES KNOCKED A NEW INVENTION OFF A TABLE!

WHEN: 1943

WHERE: UNITED STATES OF AMERICA

WHAT HAPPENED? WE GOT THE SLINKY!

It's not just humans who get dizzy on boats. Equipment doesn't like being shaken about either. For years and years, sailors really wanted an invention that could hold all their sensitive tools still on rough seas.

Back in the 1940s, inventor Richard James came up with a spring that was designed to help keep things in place. One day, **BY ACCIDENT**, he knocked his new invention off a table. Normally, when you knock something off a table you get shouted at by a grown-up because you might have broken something or made a mess. Richard was already a grown-up so I guess he'd have to shout at himself. **HOWEVER**, the spring didn't break or make a mess – it did something much more impressive. It **'WALKED'** down a pile of books that happened to be underneath it then coiled itself back up. Richard had invented the Slinky!

I DIDN'T KNOCK THE VASE OVER! I MADE A NEW PUZZLE!

Richard showed his wife, Betty, and they knew they had something that could make a lot of money. Once they perfected the design, it was a **SPRINGBOARD** to success! In 1945, it was **THE TOY** to get at Christmas. Since then, hundreds of millions have been sold. You probably have a Slinky in your house somewhere.

Just think, if there had been no **FAIL** there would probably be no Slinky and children would not have spent decades playing with a little coiled spring that could walk down stairs by itself. Thank you, Richard James, for knocking your invention off the table and giving us a lovely, wobbly, springy thing.

RATING:

1

You have to be incredibly open-minded to invent an awesome new toy when you had no intention of doing so. It just goes to show that you should keep your eyes peeled for fails at all times!

THE FAIL: CAR MAKERS REALISED A FANTASTIC INVENTION WAS FANTASTIC FAR TOO LATE

WHEN: 1903

WHERE: UNITED STATES OF AMERICA

WHAT HAPPENED? WE CAN NOW DRIVE IN THE RAIN!

The first cars were invented in the early twentieth century. For a long time, they did not have windscreen wipers, so there was no way to clear rain from their windows. People had to keep stopping to get out of their car and wipe their windows down. Can you imagine? It would be much quicker to get out and walk.

Mary Anderson was an estate developer and landlord. After she experienced a journey in a trolley car (which is a bit like a tram) being interrupted over and over again by the driver stopping to wipe his windows during bad weather, she thought she would become an inventor too. There had to be a better way to drive in the rain and snow!

She set to work on a solution and came up with windscreen wipers that drivers could move themselves, using a lever that was on the dashboard of the car. She thought the design was so good, she even applied for a patent so she could record the design and be known as the inventor. However, patents run out after a certain period of time, so she needed a car maker to believe in her quickly!

She told everyone about the design but no one wanted to listen. Some people think this was because she was a woman and a business-person. In those days it wasn't common to see a woman who was so independent, and many men in charge didn't like the idea of a woman knowing better than them. They told her that her wiper design would distract drivers and cause accidents. Personally, I can't think of anything more distracting than having to get out of your car every thirty seconds to wipe rain from a window!

Eventually, the car makers saw sense and started to build cars with wipers that were very similar to the ones Mary designed. Sadly, by this point, Mary's patent had run out, and she was never paid for her work. An **EPIC FAIL** indeed.

Even though no one believed in Mary's design, she was still smart enough to record the design in the American patent office and tell everyone she could about it. The **EPIC FAIL** of the car makers didn't stop her, and her belief in her design and willingness to share it with the world has given us an essential invention.

RATING:

It was an EPIC FAIL for Mary Anderson's design to be ignored. She made no money and got very little credit. We've giving her some credit now though! Thank you, Mary, for helping us drive safely in our cars on rainy and snowy days, with your epic invention.

THE FAIL: A COMPANY INVENTED UNPOPULAR, OVERPRICED TECHNOLOGY!

WHEN: 1970S TO 2000S!

WHERE: USA

WHAT HAPPENED? STEVE JOBS BUILT ONE OF THE BIGGEST TECHNOLOGY COMPANIES IN THE WORLD AND IT'S STILL GOING STRONG!

Steve Jobs is the co-founder of Apple. Not the fruit, the **COMPANY**! Their inventions have changed the way we listen to music, speak to each other and even tell the time. Now, Apple is a phenomenally successful company, and that is largely down to Steve Jobs. But did you know, he had some pretty **EPIC FAILS** before Apple became the company it is today?

Jobs founded the company with his friend Steve Wozniak all the way back in 1976. In 1983 they released a computer called Lisa. It cost $10,000 and no one bought it – because it cost $10,000. **EPIC FAIL** number one!

Steve's colleagues grew frustrated with making expensive computers no one wanted to buy and he was fired from his own company. Getting fired from the company you started has to be **EPIC FAIL** number two. There's no coming back from that, right? Wrong!

Steve still had some money and he invested in a little company called Pixar. They made computers that were **EXCELLENT** at making cartoons. Steve tried to sell these computers to people to use in their homes. Not many people wanted to buy them because it's much easier to watch cartoons than to make them! Yep, **EPIC FAIL** number three. But he still saw the potential in the machines.

Luckily for Steve, in 1997 Apple asked him to return. He had finally realised people would pay good money for technology, but it had to **LOOK GOOD**. He became interested in beautifully designed products that people would want to have in their homes or carry around. The new technology he inspired and invented, like the iMac, iPod and iPhone flew off the shelves.

Oh, and remember those machines he tried to flog for Pixar? They were used to make *Toy Story* in 1995, the first animated film to be made completely on a computer. Investing in Pixar wasn't such an **EPIC FAIL** after all! They were much better at making films than making computers!

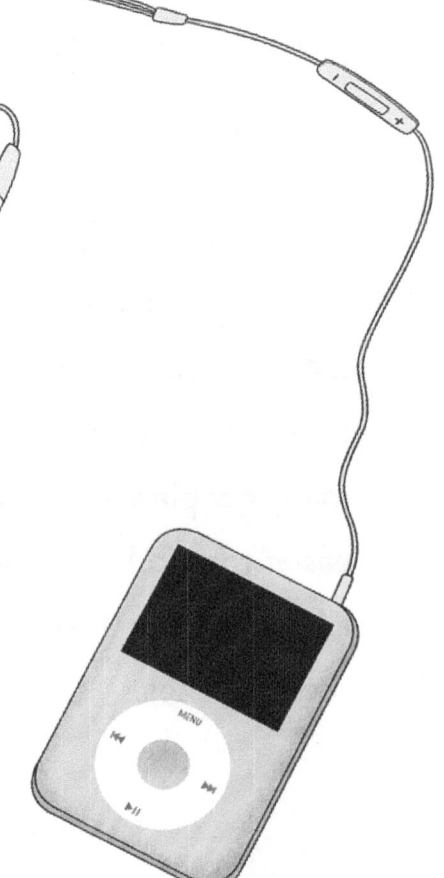

RATING:

1

Steve Jobs' genius will go down in history because the belief he had in his own inventions was unbelievable. Despite every product that didn't work, he never gave up, as he knew he just needed to keep going. By the time he joined Apple again in 1997, he had been designing and launching products for over twenty years. With that kind of 'can do' attitude, he was destined for success.

Real Fail or Fake Fail?

STEVE JOBS ONCE SAID 'I HATE FAILING! IT'S THE WORST THING EVER!'

Find the answer on page 237.

THE FAIL: A WRONG THINGY WAS PUT INTO A NEW DEVICE

WHEN: 1957

WHERE: UNITED STATES OF AMERICA

WHAT HAPPENED? THE PACEMAKER WAS INVENTED!

DID YOU KNOW that electricity makes your heart beat? The Marvel superhero Iron Man doesn't seem so special now, does he? Lots of people are battery powered!

Because we know our hearts use electricity to keep beating, some very clever people invented something called a 'pacemaker'. It is able to fix the electrical signals in people's hearts when they don't work as well as they should. The problem was, the first pacemakers were huge machines that were too big for people to carry around.

They also had to be plugged into a plug socket in a wall. If you used one, you'd need a really, really, really long cable to be able to leave the house!

One day an inventor called Wilson Greatbatch – who has a **GREAT NAME** – had a go at making a better pacemaker. He was **EXPERIMENTING** with an invention that could record people's heartbeats because he needed lots of data about heartbeats for his research. This device was meant to **RECORD** electrical rhythms. However, Greatbatch mistakenly used a part in his invention that **SENT OUT** electrical pulses. The exact opposite of what he had wanted to do! What an **EPIC FAIL!**

Did Wilson Greatbatch take his device apart and start again? **HE DID NOT!** This **EPIC FAIL** sparked Greatbatch's imagination, because guess what? His device was making electricity, but it didn't even have a battery! Maybe he had stumbled on to something that could be used as a pacemaker that didn't have to be plugged in? And maybe it was small enough for someone to carry around?

He used his accidental discovery to design a new pacemaker that surgeons could place **INSIDE** the body of patients. It was first used in 1960 and **IT WORKED**! All of the pacemakers that we use today are the result of a **FANTASTIC FAIL.**

It's now a life-saving device used by millions of people all around the world who have heart problems. It just goes to show, you can't **BEAT** a good fail! Wilson, we give you our **HEARTFELT** thanks!

RATING:

All mistakes have the potential to lead to a success. It would have been very easy for Greatbatch to take his machine apart and start again, but because he **KEPT HIS FINGER ON THE PULSE** and knew about all the problems existing pacemakers had, he was quick to see his mistake might lead to an awesome invention. With an open mind like that, you can **HEARTILY** solve any problem!

Fails for Thought

What kind of qualities do you think you need to have to spot a fantastic failure? Maybe you need to be cool and calm? Do you think positive thinking can help make a fail fabulous?

CHAPTER THREE

EPIC FAILS THAT LED TO SURPRISING DISCOVERIES

It's easy to think of **FAILS** as bad things. But that isn't always the case! Sometimes, an **EPIC FAIL** can lead to **BRAND NEW INFORMATION**. That's why it's important not to panic when something doesn't go to plan. You may have had an accident, but you might have stumbled across a brilliant discovery! All of the examples in this chapter will prove to you that **EPIC FAILS** are not the end of the world.

THE FAIL: A SCIENTIST WENT ON HOLIDAY WITHOUT CLEARING UP HIS LABORATORY

WHEN: 1928

WHERE: LONDON, UNITED KINGDOM

WHAT HAPPENED? A LIFE-SAVING DRUG WAS DISCOVERED!

Before I go on holiday, I always make sure my house is clean so I don't have work to do when I get home. In 1928, a Scottish scientist called Alexander Fleming went on holiday. He clearly didn't believe in my little life hack, and he left his **LABORATORY** in St Mary's Hospital in London a bit messy.

He happened to be working with bacteria that he was growing on Petri dishes. Petri dishes are

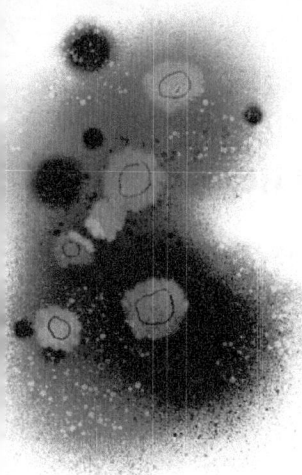

little plastic dishes that contain a gel that bacteria like to grow on. They are easy to put under a microscope and because they're like little jars, the bacteria you grow can't escape. Leaving his Petri dishes on his workbench, Alexander went to enjoy his hols.

When he returned, the dishes were full of mould. **YUCK!** What an **EPIC FAIL.** Who wants to come back from holiday to that? If I had come back to a sink full of mouldy dishes, or mouldy socks, I would have washed up **IMMEDIATELY**! But Alexander didn't, because he **NOTICED** something. There seemed to be no bacteria growing around the mould that had formed.

Alexander studied the mould and discovered that it had been able to kill the kind of bacteria that makes people sick. He named it **PENICILLIN** and after years of further research, it became the world's first human-made **ANTIBIOTIC**.

It changed the world as infections and illnesses that used to make us very sick could now be cured. **WOO HOO!** We still use it to treat many kinds of illness today. And it was all discovered because Alexander didn't tidy up his lab.*

RATING:

1

Calling penicillin an 'awesome' discovery is actually an understatement. It has saved countless lives! Even now, when you have a bacterial infection, you might be given antibiotics and get sent back to school before you miss too much of it. Which is definitely a good thing we have to thank Alexander Fleming and his epic fail for. Yippee!

---

*Please don't use Alexander's **EPIC FAIL** as an excuse not to tidy up. We only want to grow mould on petri dishes, not smelly socks!

THE FAIL: A SCIENTIST DIDN'T WASH HIS HANDS VERY WELL BEFORE EATING

WHEN: 1877

WHERE: RUSSIA

WHAT HAPPENED? HE DISCOVERED HOW TO MAKE THINGS SWEET WITHOUT USING SUGAR

It is very important to wash your hands properly before you eat food. Especially if you have to touch lots of strange and funky substances for your job – like scientists often do. A scientist called Constantin Fahlberg, who had spent the day working hard in his laboratory, **FAILED** to do this before he ate his dinner one evening. But he noticed something about his food that night – it was really sweet. He realised he must be tasting something he'd touched in his laboratory. Urrrgh, disgusting!

A lot of people might have felt a bit queasy after that, but, being a scientist, Fahlberg couldn't ignore the fact he liked the taste of his unwashed hands. He went back to his lab and realised that the taste came from something he had made by accident after an **EXPERIMENT**. He did more tests and discovered something that could be used instead of sugar. He called this new sweet-tasting substance saccharine.

People knew at the time that sugar wasn't very healthy. Sugar is terrible for your teeth and too much of it can be bad for your health. Constantin had a brainwave! He immediately thought that saccharine could help people who liked sweet things avoid the effects of too much sugar.

Now people use saccharine as an alternative to sugar in all kinds of food and drink – from diet versions of fizzy pop to chewing gum. And we have to thank someone who didn't wash their hands properly before eating for the discovery. Thank you, **EPIC FAIL**!

RATING:

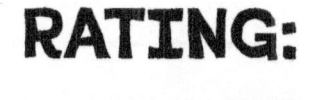

1

Constantin Fahlberg could have dismissed the sweet taste on his hands. But being curious helped him get to the bottom of the mystery taste, and it proves that it's always worth asking questions. Discovering an alternative to sugar sure is sweet!

Real Fail or Fake Fail?

A KING FAILED TO WIN A BATTLE AFTER AN OLD LADY THREW A SHOE AT HIM.

Find the answer on page 237.

THE FAIL: ALBERT EINSTEIN FAILED AN ENTRANCE EXAM, THEN DIDN'T DO VERY WELL AT SCHOOL

WHEN: EARLY TWENTIETH CENTURY

WHERE: GERMANY AND SWITZERLAND

WHAT HAPPENED? HE DISCOVERED THE MYSTERIES OF THE UNIVERSE

Albert Einstein is one of the most famous scientists in the world. He was excellent at **PHYSICS**, which means he was interested in how things move, or what things are made of. Physics can help us understand huge ideas, like space and time. It hasn't invented us a robot that can fold our clothes and put them away, but we'll get there!

Nowadays we think of Einstein as a success but that wasn't always the case. He experienced many **EPIC FAILS** on his path to greatness. Firstly, he wasn't able to speak well until he was four. Most children are expected to be speaking a little bit by the time they turn two! So, he didn't get off to the greatest start . . .

When he was sixteen, he failed an entrance exam for the school he wanted to go to. That might sound like an **EPIC FAIL** but he studied hard for one more year and took it again – and passed! **WOO HOO!**

But then, more disaster. The whole time he was there, the teachers didn't think much of him and he was not considered to be a great student. He graduated from this school, but not with very good grades. You would forgive him for thinking this was an **EPIC FAIL** because it meant he couldn't get a good job in a university or laboratory. Instead, he found himself working at the Swiss patent office.

However, fear not – it wasn't an **EPIC FAIL** at all! It turned into an **EPIC OPPORTUNITY**. The Swiss patent office was perfect for Einstein! You see, a patent office is where people send their designs and ideas so they can make sure no one else takes the credit for them. Einstein got to look at the work of other people and he used this as inspiration to make his own scientific discoveries. Everyone at the patent office was incredibly impressed by his dedication to new ways of thinking. Finally, he had a place where his genius could be recognised.

A full nine years after he graduated, he finally became a professor. You might think that's a long time to wait before you get your dream job, but is it? All the work Einstein did in the patent office helped him become the brilliant scientist we know him to be, and he made loads of epic discoveries that changed the way we see the entire universe.

RATING:

1

Einstein was a genius. He may have taken a long time to speak, but he more than made up for lost time. His journey is proof that the path to success isn't always the same one that everyone else takes.

THE FAIL: AN EXPERIMENT WITH A NEW MATERIAL WENT WRONG!

WHEN: 1965

WHERE: AMERICA AND GERMANY

WHAT HAPPENED? WE DISCOVERED MATERIAL THAT COULD STOP BULLETS!

SPOILER ALERT

One of my favourite films, *Back to the Future*, ends with the character Doc Brown's life being saved because he's wearing a bulletproof vest. But did you know that the Kevlar – a synthetic fibre – used to make bulletproof vests bulletproof was discovered after an **EPIC FAIL**?

An American inventor called Stephanie Kwolek was working as a chemist for a big company in America.

She was trying to make car tyres lighter. Tyres in the 1960s were made using steel, which is quite a heavy metal! It meant they couldn't move as quickly as people wanted and this meant cars couldn't go very fast.

One day, Kwolek was experimenting with a liquid that could be turned into a solid material to be used in tyres. She had intended to make a clear, thick solution from her experiment because she thought that's what her magic car-tyre-material-stuff would probably look like.

Instead, her experiment ended up with a very runny, cloudy mixture – the complete opposite of what she wanted! Most people would have seen this as an **EPIC FAIL**, thrown away the dodgy batch and started again. But Kwolek did not see the harm in testing what this cloudy stuff could do. She soon realised she had made something far stronger than anything that existed at that time. It was a very strong, lightweight and heat-resistant synthetic fibre. She had discovered Kevlar – by mistake!

She made lots and lots more Kevlar and now it's used by the police, the army – anyone who needs to protect themselves from gunshots.

RATING:

1

Kevlar exists because Stephanie Kwolek didn't panic when she made a mistake. She just experimented more to see where her EPIC FAIL might lead her – it turns out it led to an epic discovery.

CHAPTER FOUR

EPIC FAILS DURING WARS

The last thing anybody fighting a war needs is an **EPIC FAIL** that makes everything worse! Unfortunately, wars throughout history are full of **FAILS**. Making decisions during a war is a very difficult thing. There is a lot of pressure because if you make the wrong move, it can have **DEVASTATING** consequences. And don't forget – your enemy is always trying to outsmart you. It can be very easy to think you are making the right decision when, really, you are playing into your opponent's hands.

So, **EPIC FAILS** during wars often have **EPIC CONSEQUENCES**. This is why fails during wars fully deserve their own chapter. Go on, then! What are you waiting for? **CHARRRRRGE** into chapter four!

BOUDICA THOUGHT THAT SIZE DOES MATTER

WHEN: 61 CE

WHERE: SOUTHERN ENGLAND

WHAT HAPPENED? THE ROMANS TOOK OVER THE BRITISH ISLES FOR 350 YEARS!

The Romans invaded Britain in 4 CE. After that, King Prasutagus of the Iceni – a tribe that lived in Southern England – ruled on behalf of the Romans and generally allowed the Romans and Iceni people to get along. However, everything changed when he died and the Romans decided to take over the Iceni kingdom. **HOW RUDE!** Boudica, his queen, became the ruler of the Iceni, but she did not want the Romans to be in charge.

In 61 CE, she gathered her army of 120,000 men and raided three Roman settlements. Nowadays, these settlements are known as Colchester, St Albans and London.

Having so many fighters should have made it easy to get rid of the Romans, right? I'm afraid that's wrong! The rebellion ended up being an **EPIC FAIL** because Boudica decided to attack three different towns that aren't very close together, so her army was very stretched out. Also, even though there were lots of people fighting for Boudica, they were not as organised or well-equipped as the Roman army.

The final battle took place in around 61 CE, near Warwickshire in England. Some historians think it took place near a Roman road called Watling Street, and that's why it's known as, you've guessed it, the Battle of Watling Street. In the end, Boudica was outsmarted by Gaius Suetonius Paulinus, the wily Roman commander she was facing. He led Boudica's soldiers into a trap – a narrow battleground in which Boudica's huge army became an easy target.

Instead of having space to fight, they were all squished together.

Boudica's rebellion has to be classed as an **EPIC FAIL** because it was the start of the Roman Empire controlling Britain. And they were in charge for around 350 years. She's still known as a courageous and fearless leader, but she's also known for this **EPIC FAIL** too.

RATING:

3

Maybe it wasn't Boudica's fault that the Romans took over the British Isles. They had far superior weapons and were much more organised. With such advantages, it was probably only a matter of time before they straightened up our roads!

THE FAIL: TROOPS LEFT THEIR SAFE SPACE TO ATTACK PEOPLE THEY WERE TRYING TO DEFEAT!

WHEN: 642 CE

WHERE: PERSIA (MODERN-DAY IRAN)

WHAT HAPPENED? THE SASANIAN EMPIRE WAS ENDED!

Ever heard of the Sasanian Empire? The reason you might not know them could be because they lost the Battle of Nahāvand in 642 CE. This was a **BIG DEAL** because the Middle East completely changed soon after. And the Sasanian Empire lost that battle because of an **EPIC FAIL**!

The Sasanian Empire ruled Persia, modern-day Iran, between 224 CE and 651 CE.

In the years leading up to this battle, the Sasanian Empire was in trouble. Between 602 CE and 628 CE, they were having constant scuffles with the Byzantine Empire – remember those guys who used to run Constantinople? Then, they had a civil war between 628 CE and 632 CE. It's just one thing after another, isn't it?

New Arab forces could smell weakness and decided to take the Sasanian Empire for themselves, and in 642 CE, they launched an attack.

At Nahāvand, a city in the east of the region, around 30,000 Arab troops attacked a Sasanian army that some historians say numbered 150,000 fighters. The Sasanian troops were also in an **EXCELLENT POSITION**, hidden between two mountains. The attack didn't work. Eventually the Arab troops **GAVE UP** and walked away from the battle.

That didn't please the Sasanian troops, who wanted to keep on fighting. They left their **EXCELLENT POSITION** to try and defeat the Arab invaders for good. Unfortunately for them, they had been **TRICKED**! The Arab troops hadn't given up; they wanted the Sasanian army to leave their **EXCELLENT POSITION** so they could be successfully attacked. What an **EPIC FAIL**!

The Sasanians ended up trapped in a small space where their large numbers gave them no advantage because they were squashed in, a bit like Boudica's army. They eventually lost an epic battle and the Sasanian Empire ended soon after. One **EPIC FAIL** led to some mighty **EPIC CHANGES**!

RATING:

Standing your ground is very important. But the Sasanian Empire was in so much trouble, maybe it was only a matter of time before another great empire was going to come along and take over their lands?

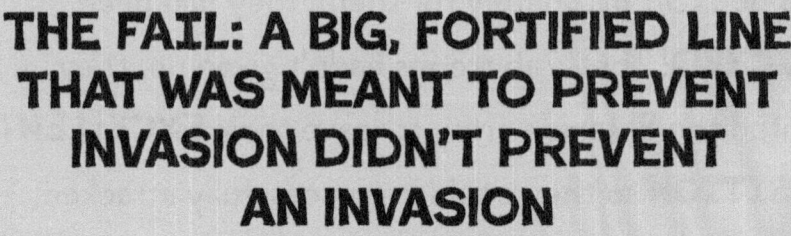

THE FAIL: A BIG, FORTIFIED LINE THAT WAS MEANT TO PREVENT INVASION DIDN'T PREVENT AN INVASION

WHEN: 1940

WHERE: FRANCE

WHAT HAPPENED? THE NAZIS INVADED FRANCE AND EVENTUALLY OCCUPIED THE COUNTRY DURING THE SECOND WORLD WAR

After the First World War ended, lots of countries in Europe were very worried about being attacked by other neighbouring countries in the future. The French military built something called the Maginot Line. It was like wall – but better! It had places to hide weapons and forts dotted along it. This super-wall was meant to deter armies from attacking France.

Unfortunately, the Maginot Line was an **EPIC FAIL** because it didn't keep the German army out. Instead of going over the wall, they just went around it instead. The super-wall turned out to be quite normal, and France fell very quickly to the German **INVASION** near the start of the Second World War.

The problem was, the wall stopped at a forest called the Ardennes. The French military thought they could get natural protection from the trees and thick vegetation. It turns out soldiers are quite good at getting though all that!

A bit like the wall around Constantinople, the Maginot Line wasn't effective against most modern weapons. It was built thinking wars would be fought like they were in the First World War, with soldiers on foot carrying guns and bayonets. After tanks were invented, going around a wall or through a forest was quite easy.

RATING:

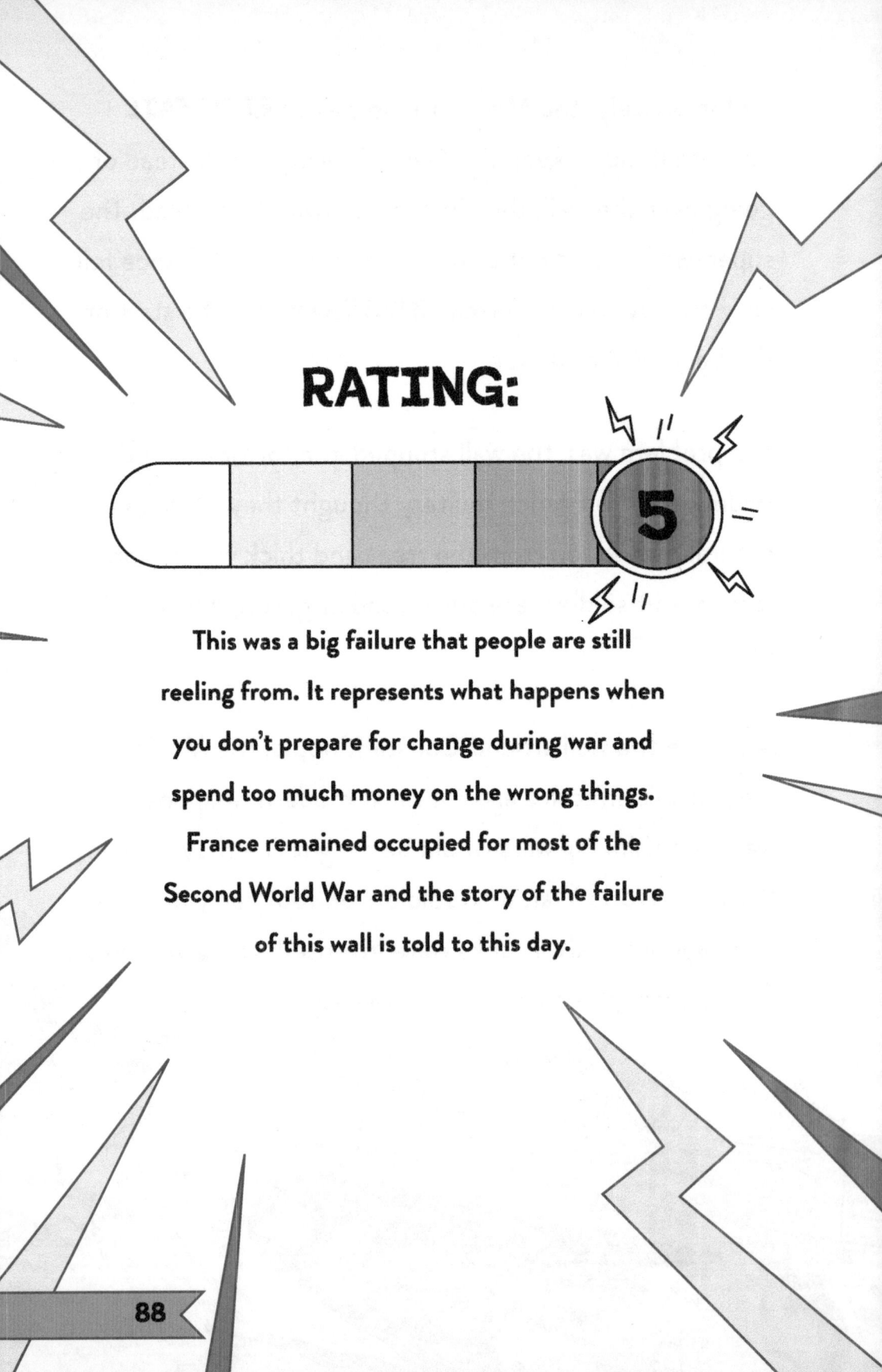

5

This was a big failure that people are still reeling from. It represents what happens when you don't prepare for change during war and spend too much money on the wrong things. France remained occupied for most of the Second World War and the story of the failure of this wall is told to this day.

THE FAIL: NAPOLEON INVADED RUSSIA, WHICH IS KNOWN FOR BEING VERY COLD!

WHEN: 1812

WHERE: MODERN-DAY POLAND AND RUSSIA

WHAT HAPPENED? NAPOLEON GOT EXILED

When an **EPIC FAIL** inspires one of the most famous pieces of classical music,* one of the world's most famous books** and a film by one of Hollywood's most famous directors,*** it's earned the right to be in the most **FAMOUS BOOK** about **EPIC FAILS**! OK, this might be the only book about **EPIC FAILS** but let's not dwell on that. Let's get on with it!

---

* The '1812 Overture' by Tchaikovsky – you'll recognise it when you hear it.
**_War and Peace_ by Leo Tolstoy – an epic book by an epic writer.
***_Napoleon_ directed by Ridley Scot – personally, I liked this film!

Napoleon Bonaparte was a leader in France who went to war with Russia in 1812. One big reason was that Russia was friendly with Britain at the time and Napoleon wasn't. Probably because they ran around telling everyone he was short, when he was actually the average height for a man of his time. (As you will know if you read *History's Most Epic Fibs!*)

Everyone told him it was a bad idea to invade Russia. He was already fighting lots of wars and was running low on money, morale and supplies. But he didn't listen.

His armies were used to 'living off the land' as they fought, and he thought while they were fighting in Russia, they could forage for food and look after themselves. Unfortunately, the land he was invading was not very fertile and it was winter, so not much was growing. All their other supplies were meant

NEXT TIME I WILL CHECK THE WEATHER FORECAST.

to be carried by horses and wagons, but the horses didn't have proper winter shoes. Eventually they couldn't keep up with the marching soldiers and so basic supplies like clothes, water and equipment for shelters, couldn't reach Napoleon's armies in time.

Before his soldiers faced a single Russian battle, they were facing hunger from the lack of food and exposure to the cold. This is definitely an **EPIC FAIL**.

When the French eventually reached Russia to fight, the Russian army retreated. When you fight a war, you expect your opponent to race to battle, not run away from it! As the Russians went back, further and further into Russia, the French army followed them. This only took them further away from the supplies that were already far behind them, and further into freezing cold temperatures. Pretty soon, the French soldiers started to perish.

Eventually, Napoleon couldn't continue to justify the losses he was facing. When it was clear there would be no French victory, he admitted defeat. To cement their victory, Russia, along with their buddies Prussia and Austria, exiled Napoleon to a small island near Italy called Elba.

An **EPIC FAIL** indeed! But it did lead to some epic music, an epic book and an epic film!

RATING:

4

Napoleon listened to no one and achieved nothing except the loss of many soldiers. EPIC FAIL! Some fails are completely avoidable and they happen because people in charge do not listen to other opinions, even when they're at war. Sometimes when you're a leader you have to listen to the experts, not pretend to be an expert!

THE FAIL: EUROPEANS INVADED ETHIOPIA THINKING ETHIOPIANS WOULD BE PUSHOVERS

WHEN: 1896

WHERE: ETHIOPIA

WHAT HAPPENED? ETHIOPIA WAS DECLARED INDEPENDENT! WOO HOO!

European nations in the nineteenth century started something called the 'Scramble for Africa'. Lots of different countries wanted to own land on the continent of Africa for resources, to give them an advantage over their enemies or to just show off.

Britain, France and Portugal had been successful in claiming land in Africa, but Italy was missing out. They had taken over what is now a small country in East Africa called Eritrea, but it was tiny compared to all the land everyone else had taken. To 'correct' this, in 1896 Italy decided to invade the country next door to Eritrea, Ethiopia.

This decision was an **EPIC FAIL**. The leader of Ethiopia at the time was Emperor Menelik II, who happened to be very good at fighting battles. He was also well liked by his friends in the area. This meant armies from all over East Africa agreed to fight with him to defeat the Italian invaders. He also made a brilliant decision: he waited. Rather than attack the Italians as soon as they entered the country, he organised all his troops and all his alliances so he would be well prepared.

It was a great plan, because by the time the Ethiopian army met the Italian army, the Ethiopian army had around 100,000 fighters. Italy had just 17,000. To beat an army that outnumbers you by that much, you need:

- Better weapons
- A better position
- Good knowledge of the land you are fighting in
- Luck!

The Italians had none of the above and they were defeated. Funnily enough, considering so many countries wanted to take over land in Africa at the time, many European countries were horrified by Italy's actions. They made sure a treaty was signed – a formal agreement – that guaranteed Ethiopia's independence. This was a very radical thing for European nations to do. As a result, even after the Scramble for Africa, Ethiopia remains the only country in Africa never to have been subjected to European or American rule.

RATING:

5

This was a **HUMUNGOUS FAIL** because if you're going to pick a fight with a country, you should probably make sure you have all the things you need to win the fight first. Also, here's a thought: a great way to avoid **EPIC FAILS** is to maybe **NOT** pick fights in the first place!

THE FAIL: AN ARMY WAS MADE TO WALK FOR AGES THEN SPLIT INTO FOUR GROUPS

WHEN: 1876

WHERE: MONTANA, UNITED STATES OF AMERICA

WHAT HAPPENED? A WHOLE ARMY GOT DEFEATED IN LESS THAN AN HOUR!

During the late 1800s in the United States of America, white American settlers were at war with Native Americans. The settlers' plan was to occupy the whole country and take over the land while Native Americans would be given areas called 'reservations' to live in. These reservations were a disaster for the Native Americans. Many of their various cultures and traditions relied on being nomadic – that means travelling around a country as a way of life – on the American plains. Native Americans tried to fight back on many occasions, and this was one of them.

The American government had promised land in a state called Dakota to the Sioux and Cheyenne Native American nations. The problem was, they had to stay on this land and they were not allowed to leave. These boundaries felt insulting. Under a leader called Sitting Bull, they decided to fight for the right to roam the plains as they wished. One by one, Native Americans decided to leave the reservations they had been ordered to stay in.

The American government saw this as an uprising and sent three large armies to stop it. One was led by General Custer. He was ordered to find the leader, Sitting Bull. It didn't take Custer long to make his first **EPIC FAIL**. To get to Sitting Bull, his army had to walk around some mountains. Thinking that would take too long, he ordered his army to walk through the mountain range, which exhausted them. Have you ever tried walking through some mountains?

They are very hilly! My legs hurt just thinking about it!

When they got to the battleground, he split his army into four smaller groups, thinking he could surround the Native Americans and overpower them. This was **EPIC FAIL** number two. All he did was make his army weak by making them attack in smaller numbers.

Custer found Sitting Bull's village and this led to his third **EPIC FAIL**. He noticed that he was seen by some of people from the village. He thought that they would be so scared of the white settlers' army, Sitting Bull would tell the villagers to scatter and run. That's a great time to attack a village! He decided to attack immediately, while the village was in a state of panic.

He could not have been more wrong. Sitting Bull and his army were happy to wait for them to attack. They had 2,000 men fighting, compared to Custer's 800 men, they had better guns and they were in a better position.

Sitting Bull defeated Custer's army within one hour. All of Custer's men were killed, including Custer himself.

The battle became known as Custer's Last Stand.

The victory celebrations for the Sioux and Cheyenne Native Americans did not last long. Once America realised how capable they were in battle, they sent more troops and ordered them to be more brutal. By 1890, almost all the Native Americans were living in reservations again. Custer's **EPIC FAIL** was fatal for his army but made the American government even more determined to take the country from Native Americans for good.

RATING:

5

Definitely a 5 – everyone died. Custer's decisions are now famous for being catastrophic. It shows the importance of respecting people on the other side in battles. Even if what you are doing is cruel and unfair, you must never underestimate the people you are fighting against.

THE FAIL: A DRIVER TOOK THE WRONG TURN WHEN DRIVING A FUTURE KING AROUND

WHEN: 1914

WHERE: BOSNIA AND HERZEGOVINA

WHAT HAPPENED? THE FIRST WORLD WAR STARTED.

This fail didn't technically happen during a war, but it happened right before one of the biggest ones. Let's take a trip back to Europe in 1914, which was a very tense time. Countries had made different alliances on the continent. Britain, France and Russia were mates and Germany and Austria-Hungary were mates, but the two groups did not get on.

There were also huge advances in military weapons that made every country more ambitious. With all the tanks and guns that were being invented, people started to wonder if they would be able to take over somebody else's country for themselves. It only needed one thing to spark a war and that thing happened to be the result of an **EPIC FAIL**!

Archduke Frankz Ferdinand was going to be ruler of the Austro-Hungarian Empire. The empire included a city called Sarajevo, in Bosnia. In 1914 the Archduke visited Sarajevo, which was a risky thing to do, as people from neighbouring Serbia didn't want Sarajevo to be ruled by the Archduke. They used all kinds of tactics, including violence, to try to end Austria-Hungary's control.

The Archduke paid no attention to the threat. He told everyone about the route of the parade he was going to take and travelled in an open-top car. In hindsight, this all sounds very reckless. He might as well have worn a T-shirt that said, 'Come and have a go if you think you're hard enough!'

Along his route, as predicted by his advisors, a bomb was thrown at his car. The bomb hit the car behind. That would have been a good time for his staff to say, 'I told you so!' But Ferdinand, for some reason, still felt safe to continue. **EPIC FAIL**.

Eventually, he came to his senses and realised that he should be driven on a different route later in the day. However, no one remembered to tell his driver. Another **EPIC FAIL**! Everyone and their auntie knew the route he was taking, including the assassin who eventually shot him. **DISASTER!**

At the time, everyone thought it was a Serbian fighting for Sarajevo that did it and one month later, Austria-Hungary declared war on Serbia in retaliation. Germany then declared war on Russia, who was an ally of Serbia. Then everyone joined in. And the First World War began.

RATING:

5

Any fail that causes a major war is going to make the fail-o-meter arrow swing! It was always likely that things were going to kick off, but this event had a massive impact. Leaders often want to look strong, and value maintaining a confident, fearless image over being safe. But in the end, this really happened because someone forgot to tell the driver to drive a different route!

THE FAIL: THE AUSTRALIAN GOVERNMENT THOUGHT IT WAS EASY TO KILL EMUS

WHEN: 1932

WHERE: AUSTRALIA

WHAT HAPPENED? EMUS BECAME A PROTECTED SPECIES!

In the 1930s, settlers in Australia were busy trying to make a home for themselves in the country. They encountered lots of wildlife that didn't really want their home to be taken over by people. Like the magnificent emu!

Emus are large birds that cannot fly, and they have lived in Australia for thousands of years. Because they are so big, they are very hungry and they used to eat lots of the crops that the settlers tried to grow. There was only one thing for the government to do: **DECLARE WAR ON THE EMUS!**

The Australian government decided 20,000 emus could be killed with machine guns. However, after one month of firing at them, only 1,000 were killed. Either emus run very fast or the shooters must have had terrible aim!

No one could have predicted how good emus were at war. (I never predicted having to write that sentence!) In one battle, the birds all ran in different directions and managed to avoid being shot. Some farmers tried to herd the emus using trucks, but the emus were too fast. And don't forget – emus are really big! One truck drove into one and it ended up doing more damage to the truck than the bird!

Eventually, the Australian government waved the white flag (not that emus would have known what the heck that meant!) and admitted defeat. The emus are now a protected species – meaning you get in trouble if you try and hunt one, and we can appreciate how truly special they are. Human vs emu. The emus won. **RESPECT!**

RATING:

5

Getting outsmarted by a bird has to be a 5. When humans decide to move to a different country, it's much better to live in harmony with the wildlife they find, rather than destroy it!

Real Fail or Fake Fail?

A **PARROT** RUINED THE FUNERAL OF AMERICA'S **SEVENTH** PRESIDENT, ANDREW JACKSON.

Find the answer on page 237.

THE FAIL: A KING WAS SO HORRIBLE HIS ARMY WOULDN'T FIGHT FOR HIM!

WHEN: 1046 BCE

WHERE: CHINA

WHAT HAPPENED? HIS DYNASTY ENDED!

If you ever ask a grown-up for something, they tend to make you say 'PLEASE' before they give it to you. This is called 'GOOD MANNERS'! It's important to have good manners, especially towards the people that you need to do things for you. If you're impolite, they may not like doing what you say.

This is exactly the problem King Di Xin had. He was the leader of the Shang DYNASTY in China in 1046 BCE and was known for being a bit of a tyrant. He collected taxes from his people and, instead of spending money for the good of the Shang, he spent a lot of money on himself.

Close to him were leaders of the Zhou – people who quite fancied running the Shang part of China for themselves. They grew in strength and numbers and decided that one day, they would be big enough and strong enough to fight the Shang armies, then take over their empire.

King Di Xin found about the Zhou's plot and he wasn't having any of it. He got all his generals together and told them that they would need to prepare to fight for his legacy.

I am not sure if he said 'please' but even if he had, after years of mistreating his people, that probably wouldn't have made much difference. His generals told him that the soldiers were busy doing something else – something Di Xin had in fact ordered them to do earlier.

Di Xin decided to make a new army out of villagers and peasants instead. However, these were perhaps the people who had suffered most. The chance of a new leader was an enticing one. Instead of fighting, they could just give up and someone else could be in charge.

And that's exactly what happened! With a lacklustre army made up of people who weren't even soldiers, King Di Xin was defeated. The Battle of Muye was the final battle and it finished with his palace being stormed. King Di Xin's head wound up on a flagpole and the Shang dynasty came to a **GRUESOME END**.

WHAT'S THE MAGIC WORD?

NOW!

RATING:

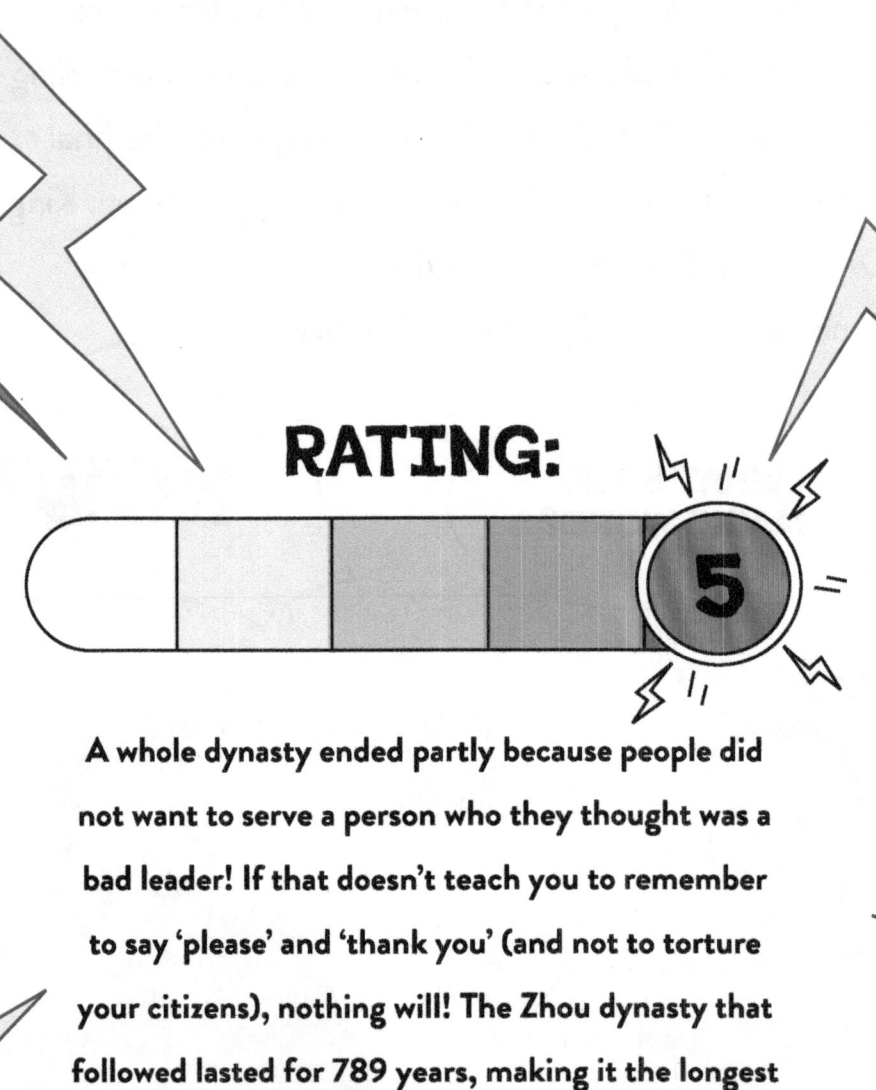

5

A whole dynasty ended partly because people did not want to serve a person who they thought was a bad leader! If that doesn't teach you to remember to say 'please' and 'thank you' (and not to torture your citizens), nothing will! The Zhou dynasty that followed lasted for 789 years, making it the longest of all the dynasties in Chinese history.

Fails for Thought

Why is it so hard to make the right decisions during a battle? There are lots of stories in this chapter – did you noticed any FAILS that were repeated in wars throughout history?

CHAPTER FIVE

EPIC FAILS THAT BROKE (OR ALMOST BROKE) SOME VERY BIG BUSINESSES

Running a business can be a good way to make lots of cash. It's also a way to run into some **EPIC FAILS**! For example, what products should you plan to sell so you can keep up with your customers? What should you do if another business comes along that might be better than yours? How are you going to keep up with new technology? These are big questions and it is **NOT EASY** to always have the right answer.

Because running a business is so risky, it's not unusual to run into an **EPIC BUSINESS FAIL**. That also means that there is **A LOT** to be learned. So, if you think you would like be the leader of a **COMPANY** one day, read on and take notes. These businesses made mistakes, so that future you doesn't have to!

THE FAIL: A COMPANY THOUGHT PEOPLE WOULD WANT VIDEOS FOREVER

WHEN: 1990S

WHERE: EVERYWHERE IN THE WORLD

WHAT HAPPENED? THE WORLD'S BIGGEST VIDEO RENTAL COMPANY WENT BUST

Years ago, before you could watch your favourite film on a laptop, tablet or streaming channel on TV, you had to watch them using something called a **VIDEO TAPE**.

A video tape looked like this:

HOWEVER, these tapes were quite expensive and also quite big. When you wanted to watch a film you didn't own, you had to **LEAVE YOUR HOUSE** and walk

to something called a **VIDEO RENTAL STORE**.

The biggest company to run these stores was called Blockbuster Video. They had over 9,000 stores, and across the world, over 50 million people were members. They were the McDonalds of the video world! But it all went wrong when the people in charge **DID NOT BELIEVE** that people would want to change the way they watched films.

Eventually DVDs started to take over from video tapes and a little company called Netflix was invented. DVDs were much smaller and much cheaper than the old video tapes, too. People were happy to buy the films they liked and were able to store the small, slim boxes in their homes.

Then, Netflix thought people would like to stream movies online. Netflix made Blockbuster an offer. For $50 million, they would operate a streaming service to help Blockbuster evolve into an online company. But Blockbuster said 'no' because they were the **BIGGEST RENTAL COMPANY IN THE WORLD**!

Eventually, Netflix built their own streaming platform and changed the way we watch film and TV. Now, they are one of the **BIGGEST STREAMING COMPANIES IN THE WORLD**! And sadly, Blockbuster doesn't exist. What a **BLOCKBUSTER FAIL**!

RATING:

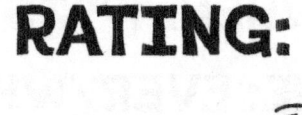

4

Blockbuster had all the help they needed to avert disaster! They were a successful business full of cash and they could have taken Netflix's offer. But they thought customers would be loyal to them no matter what. Customers are loyal to the thing that is most convenient. I admire their faith in people wanting to leave their houses to get things, but quite frankly, ordering stuff online was always going to be the future!

THE FAIL: A COMPANY WAS OBSESSED WITH CAMERA FILM

WHEN: 1990S

WHERE: EVERYWHERE

WHAT HAPPENED? NO MORE KODAK MOMENTS!

Kodak used to be the biggest photography company in the world. They made cameras and camera film and even started making movies.

Old cameras worked very differently to modern-day cameras. They needed camera film.

Camera film is a very thin plastic that used to come rolled up in a plastic container. You would put this container into your camera, then take your pictures. When your film was finished, you would take your container to a shop to have your film developed into pictures. If that sounds like a lot of work, it's because it was. Imagine having to wait **DAYS** before you can see what a picture you've taken looks like!

Fast forward a few years and Kodak invented the digital camera! But they didn't want to sell it – why?

Well, Kodak made **A LOT** of money selling camera film. They were afraid of selling digital cameras to people because they wouldn't be able to make as much money.

Also, early digital cameras were a bit rubbish. They were expensive and took terrible pictures.

However, technology improves over time. By the time Kodak realised the power of digital photography, all their competitors had snapped up most of the digital camera market before they could get a slice. What an **EPIC FAIL**.

In 2012, Kodak filed for bankruptcy, but it still exists. And guess what it makes now?

CAMERA FILM!

Lots of people who love photography **LOVE** film and it's great that Kodak is still around so this way of taking pictures isn't completely lost. Some films and TV shows are still made on old-fashioned cameras, as lots of filmmakers actually prefer it. Who knows? Maybe Kodak can make a comeback?

RATING:

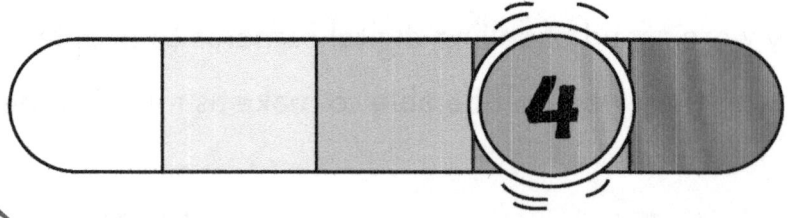

4

This was a mess that could have been avoided if Kodak weren't so fanatical about film. Like Blockbuster, they thought people were faithful to them, but really they were faithful to convenience. HOWEVER, by keeping camera film alive, photographers and filmmakers still have a company that can help them make films and take pictures the old way – which lots of people still think is better!

THE FAIL: RECORD LABELS THOUGHT THE BEATLES WEREN'T VERY GOOD AND DIDN'T SIGN THEM

WHEN: 1960S

WHERE: BRITAIN

WHAT HAPPENED? THE BEATLES BECAME THE BIGGEST BAND IN THE WORLD ANYWAY!

The Beatles were a band from Liverpool, in the United Kingdom. In the 1960s, they were the **BIGGEST BAND IN THE WORLD**.

Like all bands, they had to start at the bottom. For a long time, they were four young men playing songs in bars and clubs trying to get their big break.

They had a manager called Brian Epstein, who decided he would take his band to London to meet people who worked for record companies. He asked loads of record companies to **COME TOGETHER** for a meeting and they all turned him down. Finally, someone from a record label called Decca decided he would like to see the band play. **YAY** – their big break was on the horizon.

The Beatles travelled to North London on New Year's Day in 1962 and went to a studio that would later become the famous Abbey Road Studios. They played Decca fifteen songs and even recorded a tape for them. Then they returned to Liverpool to wait. They waited for one month. Finally, they got a response. **YAY!** Decca told them:

'Guitar groups are on the way out' and 'The Beatles have no future in show business'.

Yikes. They clearly didn't think the band were anything to **SHOUT** about. You're supposed to give **GOOD** feedback with your **BAD** feedback, Decca!

Brian Epstein didn't give up, though. He truly believed in The Beatles and went straight to another company. EMI decided to help and signed them instead. Decca continued as a company, but they missed out on **MILLIONS**. They must have been kicking themselves!

RATING:

2

We think it's a 2 because you can't sign a band you don't like. Maybe The Beatles wouldn't have been so successful if Decca had been in charge. Who knows? We're happy to 'rock and roll' with this fail!

THE FAIL: COCA-COLA CHANGED THE RECIPE OF EVERYONE'S FAVOURITE DRINK

WHEN: 1980S

WHERE: UNITED STATES OF AMERICA AND CANADA

WHAT HAPPENED? PANDEMONIUM!

I have travelled across Europe, Africa, the Caribbean and America and there is one thing I see, everywhere I go. No, not airports, though they are everywhere! I'm talking about the Coca-Cola logo. Coca-Cola is a huge company and it has been huge for a long time.

However, one day, about forty years ago, they made a decision that could have had disastrous consequences. They changed the recipe of their bestselling drink!

There was a huge advertising campaign telling everyone the old Coca-Cola was changing into the **NEW** Coca-Cola. But **NOBODY** liked it. What an **EPIC FAIL**!

Protest societies called Society for the Preservation of the Real Thing and Old Cola Drinkers of America formed and people started buying lots of the old Coca-Cola so they wouldn't run out.

Luckily, Coca-Cola managed to fix this **EPIC FAIL**. They took all the cans and bottles of New Coca-Cola from the shelves and put back the old drink with a new name: Coca-Cola Classic. The people rejoiced. They had spoken and they were listened to. They rejoiced so much, more cans and bottles of Coca-Cola Classic were sold than ever before!

Now, New Coke is only really mentioned in stories about **EPIC BUSINESS FAILS** and Coca-Cola learned a lesson: if it isn't broke, don't fix it!

RATING:

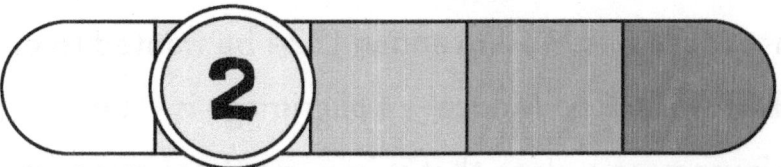

People loved Coca-Cola Classic even more than the original drink, even though it was the same drink. This FAIL worked out so well in the long run, it makes me think that it was a plan to sell more Coca-Cola all along!

THE FAIL: A RULER HANDED OUT TOO MUCH GOLD

WHEN: FOURTEENTH CENTURY

WHERE: NORTH AFRICA

WHAT HAPPENED? HE COMPLETELY MESSED UP A COUNTRY'S ECONOMY

Mansa Musa was the ruler of the Mali Empire in the fourteenth century. He is **MEGA** famous for being **MEGA** rich – in fact, he is one of the richest people to have **EVER** lived. The empire he ruled was full of gold and used to do lots of trade with countries near and far. It made him a fortune.

Mansa Musa was Muslim and in 1324 he wanted to go on a **PILGRIMAGE** to Mecca – a pilgrimage is when you go on a journey to a place that is important to your religion. It's a way to demonstrate your faith and it's seen as a very spiritual act. Visiting Mecca is considered an important journey for people who follow Islam and many try to make the journey once in their lifetime.

Mansa Musa did not travel light. He had a big entourage of around 60,000 people and thousands of camels. So, you could say he overpacked. On the way, he stopped and built mosques in different places and gave generous donations to people he met in the towns and villages. After a while, his journey became a very big deal. It was a bit like a Taylor Swift concert coming to town!

He stopped off in Cairo, Egypt, and gave away even more gold and spent lots of money. This might sound like a good thing, but the problem with gold is that it's only worth a lot when there isn't much of it about. When you have a lot of it, it goes down in value. He gave away so much gold in Egypt, he reduced its value by 25%. It took more than a decade for the economy to recover.

Really, Mansa Musa, you shouldn't have! **EPIC** generosity, but also an **EPIC FAIL**!

However, it wasn't all an **EPIC FAIL**. His pilgrimage worked as a great advertisement for his empire. Word got around about his wealth and popularity, and people began to realise how brilliant Mali was – making it even more popular for tradespeople and merchants. Maybe next time you visit your mates, give them something less valuable, like flowers!

RATING:

Mansa Musa really made sure the streets he walked on were paved with gold. Some historians think he handed out all that gold on purpose. Maybe he knew it would ruin the Egyptian economy, which would only benefit Mali. Either way, this fail helped put Mali on the map and gives us a great way to remember this wealthy but generous man!

CHAPTER SIX

EPIC FAILS THAT MADE THINGS SAFER

Some **EPIC FAILS** result in terrible things. These are **EPIC FAILS** we **HAVE** to learn from to make sure the same mistakes don't happen again and that we keep safe. Especially when some **EPIC FAILS** have cost lives. By changing the way we do things, we can save lives in the future. We're going to learn about some **EPIC FAILS** that ended up helping us change the way we do things, for the better.

THE FAIL: AN AIRSHIP WAS FILLED WITH FLAMMABLE GAS AND CRASHED

WHEN: 1937

WHERE: NEW JERSEY, UNITED STATES OF AMERICA

WHAT HAPPENED? WE STOPPED FILLING AIRSHIPS WITH FLAMMABLE GAS!

AIRSHIPS were once seen as the future of air travel and were very glamourous back in the 1930s. They were made of huge balloons with a cabin beneath them, where the pilot and passengers sat. The balloon part would be filled with a helium gas, which is very light and, crucially, not flammable.

The Hindenburg was the largest airship ever made and it was launched in Germany in 1936. However, at this time Germany was being taken over by the Nazi party – a

horrible regime that other countries in the world didn't want to do business with. For this reason, there were lots of things Germany was not allowed to buy from other countries in case they used them to make weapons. One of those things was helium.

To get around this rule, the Hindenburg was filled with hydrogen, another gas that is lighter than air. Unfortunately, unlike helium, hydrogen IS **FLAMMABLE**. This decision to use it ended up being a tragic **EPIC FAIL**.

In 1937, the Hindenburg flew across the Atlantic Ocean. It was to mark a new era in air travel. It got to America safely. However, when it set off to make the return trip, a spark caused the hydrogen to light up. It crashed after trying to take off and sadly, thirty-five people lost their lives. This **EPIC FAIL** shocked the world who witnessed it. This disaster was so tragic, people think it was responsible for airships being largely abandoned, while passenger jet planes became the most popular way for people to travel around the world.

RATING:

5

It feels so obvious now, but filling a large airship with lots of flammable gas was clearly a dangerous thing to do. Maybe they thought it was no different to planes using jet fuel, which is flammable too? After this tragedy, laws were made to make sure airships were NEVER filled with hydrogen again.

THE FAIL: SOMEONE FORGOT A VERY, VERY IMPORTANT KEY – FOR A BOX ON THE *TITANIC!*

WHEN: 1912

WHERE: THE NORTH ATLANTIC OCEAN

WHAT HAPPENED? SADLY, A SHIP THAT WAS MEANT TO BE UNSINKABLE SANK

I know what you're thinking – why would someone forgetting a key be a big deal? We've all forgotten things we need, like our PE kit. When that happens, we borrow someone else's from the dreaded leftover kit drawer.

However, this key opened a box that contained binoculars on the *Titanic* – one of the world's most famous ships – which sank in 1912 after hitting an iceberg that should have been seen by someone **LOOKING OUT** for it. Today, we know the person who was meant to be looking for dangerous things on the water did not have a pair of binoculars, which would have been quite helpful.

This was all because of an **EPIC FAIL**. The binoculars were kept in a locked box but the key for the box was not on the ship. A man called David Blair was supposed to be on the *Titanic*, but he was replaced at the last minute. When he left the ship, the key to the box was in his pocket.

When the lookouts were in the crow's nest – a bit of the boat that's quite high up so you can see for miles around – they had no tools to help them see things far away. The iceberg was seen far too late and it could not be avoided. Afterwards, survivors claimed if they had had the right tools, they would have seen the iceberg much earlier and would have been able to save the ship.

Like lots of **EPIC FAILS**, the truth is complicated.

The *Titanic* sank at night and binoculars would not have been able help in the dark. Also, it's hard to believe on a massive ship like that, with so many crew members and over 2,000 passengers, there wasn't a pair of binoculars or a telescope on the ship somewhere. No one thought to search for alternative pair when they realised they couldn't open the box. This was an **EPIC FAIL** too!

Plus, there were so many other **EPIC FAILS**. The ship wasn't designed very well, so it took on much more water than it should have when it started to sink. There were nowhere near enough lifeboats either. The unsinkable ship was, sadly, very sinkable.

RATING:

3

This forgetful EPIC FAIL doesn't have highest rating because lots of other fails contributed to this disaster. The loss of life shocked the world and laws were changed to make ships safer. It also made the ship incredibly famous, sparking many documentaries and of course the mega famous film *Titanic*. The memory of the *Titanic* will remain for a very long time. In much the same way that our journey through EPIC FAILS will go on too!

THE FAIL: AN INCY, WINCY MISTAKE WAS MADE IN A LOT OF COMPLICATED COMPUTER CODE

WHEN: 1962

WHERE: UNITED STATES OF AMERICA

WHAT HAPPENED? A SPACE ROCKET WAS DESTROYED!

The 1960s was an exciting time for exploring space. The Moon landings were being planned and the Space Race had started. America and Russia were in competition with each other to see who could build the best rockets and travel the furthest from Earth. Very groovy!

NASA built the *Mariner 1* spacecraft and launched it in 1962. It was going to be the first spacecraft to travel to Venus, study the planet and take lots of very cool pictures of the place.

Sadly, it never made it. Very soon after take-off, NASA realised that the craft was travelling dangerously off course. In fact, it looked like it was going to crash straight back down to Earth. **OH NO!** Thankfully, NASA cleverly thought to fit a 'self-destruct' button into their control room in case of an emergency like this one. To prevent anyone from getting hurt, they made the difficult decision to press it before the craft could plummet to the ground and cause harm. Not only was this an **EPIC FAIL** – it was an **EPIC FAIL** seen by the world.

Engineers **HAD** to find out what had gone wrong. And they did! It turned out it was a tiny mistake in just one of the thousands of lines of software **CODE** that the rocket needed to work. This was the actual mistake they found:

R instead of $\overline{R}$

Can you spot the difference? It's tiny!

Luckily, if you fail to prepare, you prepare to fail, and NASA had a backup plan: the fantastically named *Mariner 2*! After double (and triple) checking the software coding the second time round, they launched it later in the same year and it became the first spacecraft to visit Venus.

RATING:

2

This gets a 2 rating because NASA at least prepared for the possibility of failing with their very handy 'self-destruct' button! This EPIC FAIL forced NASA to invent a way for small, tiny mistakes to be made without confusing spaceships, and it made all their future space adventures possible. Without these new ways of working, who knows if NASA would have been able to send anyone to the Moon and back? It changed everything about the way we conduct space missions and think about safety.

THE FAIL: SOMEONE LEFT AN OVEN ON – WE THINK!

WHEN: 1666

WHERE: LONDON

WHAT HAPPENED? LOTS OF LONDON BURNED DOWN, BUT IT WAS REBUILT AGAIN!

The Great Fire of London happened in 1666 and it was a **HUGE CATASTROPHE**. It destroyed 13,200 houses, 87 churches, including St Paul's Cathedral, the Royal Exchange and Guildhall (a big, important building where big and important people used to meet in the olden days!). That is a lot of damage.

The fire started at a bakery on Pudding Lane and people **THINK** it was from a stray flame or spark from the bakery's oven. The baker survived and, a bit like Julius Caesar and the Great Library of Alexandria, claims that it wasn't started by him! He said there was a fire earlier in the day, but swore he put it out. We'll never know what really happened, but we do know the fire that devastated London started from that bakery.

There were lots of **EPIC FAILS** that led to such a devastating fire so it's not very fair to blame the baker alone. Buildings were mostly made of wood, which burns! They were also covered in thatch, which burns even more quickly than wood. And then they were coated in something called 'pitch', which is like a sticky tar, to make them a bit more watertight.
Guess what? Pitch is very flammable too.

All of this, plus the fact that buildings were tightly packed together and overcrowded, meant the fire spread incredibly quickly.

After all the **EPIC FAILS** that led to this fire spreading so quickly, things had to change. The bits of London that burned down were rebuilt with wider streets and people started to use more brick, instead of only wood.

Clever people started offering fire insurance as a way to make money. Building owners would pay insurance to people who would come and put out a fire if one started. Unfortunately, if you didn't pay, they would let your building burn. Yikes. Thankfully, the fire brigades that came about later were less ruthless and they helped everyone out!

In 1677, a monument called, ahem, Monument, was built to mark the spot where the fire started. You can visit it today as it's still standing. I think everyone liked it except the baker. Who wants a reminder that your oven probably started a fire that burned down lots of London?

RATING:

2

You might find this one too low because a big chunk of London burned down! However, we think it was just a matter of time before a big fire started. Lots of people used fires in their homes and the city was being built using things that burned easily. Was it the baker's fault? Or was it an accident waiting to happen? Either way, changing the way we build things has kept us safer in the long run.

THE FAIL: A BRIDGE WAS TOO FLEXIBLE

WHEN: 1940

WHERE: WASHINGTON STATE, UNITED STATES OF AMERICA

WHAT HAPPENED? THE FLEXIBLE BRIDGE COLLAPSED!

What are your favourite bridges? Don't look at me like that – everyone has their favourite bridges!

Mine are the Golden Gate Bridge in San Francisco, Tower Bridge in London and Brooklyn Bridge in Brooklyn – of course! These bridges are extremely famous and if you look for pictures, it's very likely you will instantly recognise them. You see, bridges are cool! The Tacoma Narrows Bridge would probably be just as famous, if it hadn't fallen down in 1940. Considered an engineering masterpiece of its day, it was the third longest suspension bridge in the world. **BUT** it's futuristic design couldn't withstand the wind and it collapsed on 7 November, just months after opening on 1 July 1940.

An extremely **EPIC FAIL**. And it was all because it had a terrible design.

People realised something was wrong with the design while it was being made. Construction workers gave it the nickname 'Galloping Gertie' because they noticed that it would sway unusually in the wind. If I was building a bridge, I would prefer one that I could call Stay Put Stan!

However, people weren't worried because the bridge was actually **SUPPOSED** to be a bit bendy. They thought if it was flexible, it would stay upright in high winds. Unfortunately, the design was never properly tested. All the flexibility ended up stretching the cables that held it in place. Once the cables snapped, it was impossible for the bridge to stay up.

Miraculously, even though the whole bridge fell down, nobody lost their life.

This **EPIC FAIL** changed the way we build bridges. Engineers still study the mistakes that were made with this bridge, and it now lives in the pages of bridge building textbooks. I imagine under chapters with names like, **'HOW NOT TO BUILD A BRIDGE'**!

The design of this bridge was an **EPIC FAIL** but since then we've learned so much. The suspension bridges we build today are bigger and stronger than ever before.

RATING:

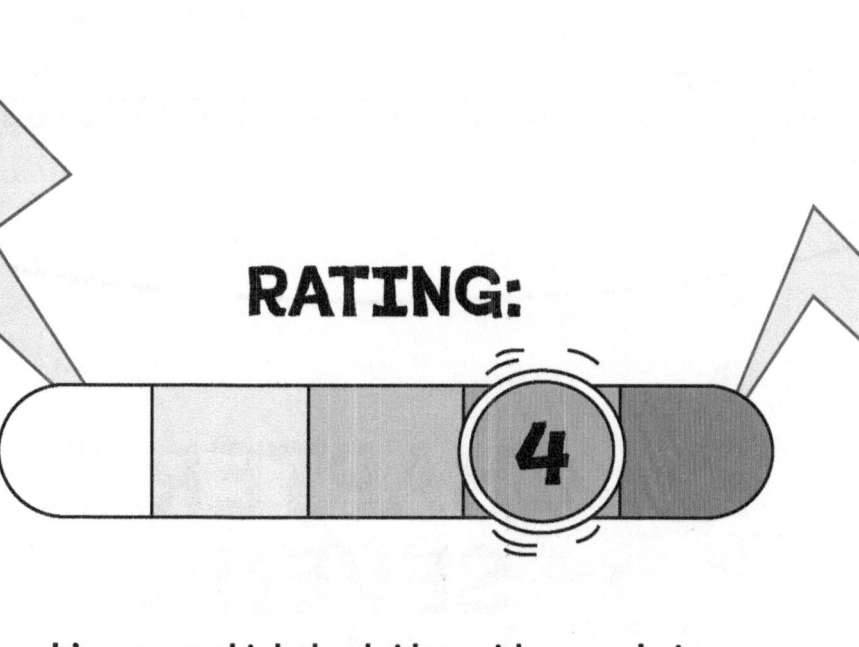

It's crazy to think that bridges with a new design could be built without testing, and that's why this gets such a high rating. It's a miracle no one lost their life. But we learned our lesson and now we have even bigger, more spectacular suspension bridges all over the world.

CHAPTER
SEVEN

EPIC FAILS
AND DOOMED
ATTEMPTS

It is important to **TRY YOUR BEST** when you do something. But it's also important to work out if your plan is doomed to fail from the beginning, or if it could have negative effects on other people. It doesn't always prevent an **EPIC FAIL**, but better to have thought about it before putting in all the effort! Here's a collection of **EPIC FAILS** where people really tried oh so hard – whether they should have done or not!

THE FAIL: ONE COUNTRY ATTEMPTED TO COLONISE ANOTHER!

WHEN: 1695 TO 1700

WHERE: SCOTLAND AND PANAMA

WHAT HAPPENED? THE COUNTRY RAN OUT OF MONEY AND EVENTUALLY HAD TO FORM A UNION WITH ITS RIVAL.

In the 1600s, countries in Europe were on a mission to get rich quick. They did try to work hard and invent stuff, but they also decided to go around the world, take over countries for themselves and claim ownership of the resources. They even tried to settle in these countries and build **NEW** countries for their own people to live in. These places are still known as 'the New World'.

In those days, the United Kingdom didn't exist. Wales, England and Scotland were all separate countries. Scotland was a small country but wanted to get rich like

England, so they came up with a plan. They would take over a bit of land in Central America called Darien and get rich from that.

Lots of people in Scotland believed in this brilliant plan and ordinary people were encouraged to give their money to the government to help. They recruited sailors and explorers and spent lots of cash on boats to Darien. Unfortunately, when they got there, they realised taking over a land, its people and its resources isn't as easy as it sounds – or OK in the slightest!

There were lots of exotic creatures in Darien that were extremely dangerous. There were also tropical diseases. Plus, people from Spain and England, who were in the area first, gave the Scots no help whatsoever.

Eventually, they had to give up and go back home. Everyone who invested in the Darien Plan lost their money and the government lost all their money too. What an **EPIC FAIL**. In 1707, Scotland decided it couldn't recover, and this is one of the many reasons it joined the United Kingdom.

RATING:

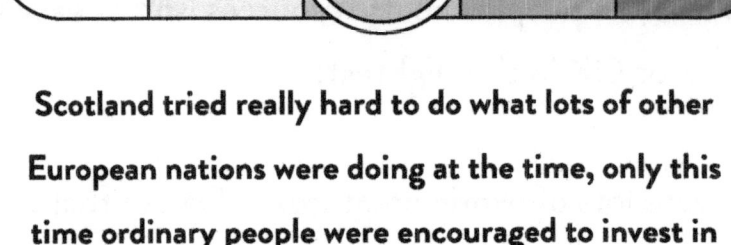

Scotland tried really hard to do what lots of other European nations were doing at the time, only this time ordinary people were encouraged to invest in the scheme and lost all their money. It then made a union with England more likely.

In the early 1600s, the king of Sweden was a powerful man called King Gustav II Adolf. He was so feared he earned the nickname 'Lion of the North'. Very impressive! To show off how powerful he was, he decided to build a **MASSIVE BOAT** for everyone to look at and think, 'Woah what a powerful guy!' It was called the *Vasa* and he wanted it to be the most incredible ship in Europe, maybe even the world.

He asked a well-known and experienced ship builder, Henrik Hybertsson, to help him design and build his super-boat. Sadly, Henrik died just a year into construction and other people, who had much less experience, had to finish it without his supervision.

Still, in 1627, the magnificent boat was finished. It was almost 70 meters long and almost 50 meters high. It had all sorts of extras – cannons (very useful for a boat!), hundreds of sculptures (not so useful) and a climbing frame (OK, it didn't have that!).

Unfortunately, the ship builders put too much effort into making sure the *Vasa* looked good, and not enough effort into making sure it could float, which is what a boat needs to do. When the finished ship finally made it to the quay at the royal palace, its captain was nervous. The boat was clearly unstable and didn't look like it would get very far. But the Lion of the North did not listen to his captain and ordered the 'best ship in the world' to be launched.

The 'best ship in the world' sailed exactly 1,300 metres before it sank. Its huge masts and heavy statues were blown over by a strong wind and water began to flood through all the holes that were meant for all the cannons. An **EPIC FAIL** indeed.

Over 300 years later, in 1961, the ship was rescued from the sea floor and you can see it today in Stockholm. It's exactly where it belongs – a museum. The *Vasa* is a beautiful thing to look at, but not so good for sailing. What should have been an **EPIC SAIL** turned into an **EPIC FAIL**!

RATING:

4

Great leaders tend to be vain and think about their image when they are building things. Lots of time and effort was put into this ship but really, they should have made sure they covered the practical things first. That ship was doomed from the off!

THE FAIL: AN EXPLORER DIDN'T HAVE THE RIGHT EQUIPMENT IN THE HOSTILE ENVIRONMENT OF ANTARCTICA

WHEN: 1910

WHERE: THE SOUTH POLE

WHAT HAPPENED? HE BECAME THE SECOND PERSON TO WALK TO THE SOUTH POLE

In 1910, Captain Robert Falcon Scott decided he wanted to walk to the South Pole. This is the most southern place on Earth and it is one of the coldest places on the planet.

Scott was a seasoned explorer, so he prepared for a long, difficult trip. He brought sledges and horses, which were meant to help him and his team travel long distances in the freezing conditions. Sadly, horses deal with the cold about as well as humans (which is not very well!) and they could not complete the journey.

The men had to walk by themselves.

It took them months. But guess what? They made it!
However, they couldn't celebrate when they got there
because they realised someone got there before them.
His name was Roald Amundsen. He was Norwegian and
much more experienced at travelling in snow and cold
weather. He used dogs, which are better suited to the
cold, and skis – which travel faster than heavy sledges.
He beat Scott by a whole month.

Deflated, Scott and his explorers started to return
home. By now their food had run out, they were tired,
and then the weather became even more terrible. They
never made it back home.

Years later, people looking for him found his
expedition party and their diaries. He and his team had
written down all their experiences and they are now
remembered for being brave, ambitious and determined.
They didn't make it, but because of their **EPIC FAIL**
this still became one of the most famous expeditions
in the world.

RATING:

2

Captain Robert Falcon Scott and his team tragically didn't make it home so you might think this is a really low score. But the fact they made it to the South Pole with such poor equipment tells us what fantastic explorers they were. Scott's bravery and ambition has led to his story being retold in books, films and documentaries. Plus, we learned so much from his journey it helped many more people travel to Antarctica to learn more about its icy, hostile environment, and the planet itself.

THE FAIL: AN OXYGEN TANK EXPLODED ON A SPACESHIP!

WHEN: 1970

WHERE: SPACE! SOMEWHERE BETWEEN EARTH AND THE MOON

WHAT HAPPENED? ASTRONAUTS DIDN'T MAKE IT TO THE MOON AND GOT STUCK IN SPACE FOR A BIT!

Apollo 13 was NASA's third attempt to visit the Moon. This time, it was the turn of three astronauts: Jack Swigert, Jim Lovell and Fred Haise, to visit the lunar surface.

Lots of people joked about '13' being an unlucky number but you need to be really good at science and engineering to send people to the Moon, so you're not likely to care about that kind of stuff.

Apollo 13 was made up of a rocket, which would take them into space, and a lunar module, which would land them on the Moon. The rocket launched 11 April 1970, and for two days everything was going fine, until the astronauts heard the worst thing you want to hear when you're in space: an explosion! Jack Swigert uttered lines that became super famous:

'HOUSTON, WE HAVE A PROBLEM!'

An oxygen tank had blown up and their spacecraft could not continue to travel. They were no longer on a mission to get to the Moon. They were on a mission to get back home to Earth safely!

They didn't know this at the time, but it was a wire in the oxygen tank that had exploded. It had been damaged during a repair back on Earth, which was an **EPIC FAIL** too!

In the end, someone had the genius idea for the astronauts to use the lunar module like a lifeboat that they could travel back to Earth in. It was a tremendous effort from everyone involved and with help from Mission Control, they travelled back home unharmed.

They **FAILED** to get to the Moon but the story of resilience, working together, being clever and remaining very calm under pressure wowed the world.

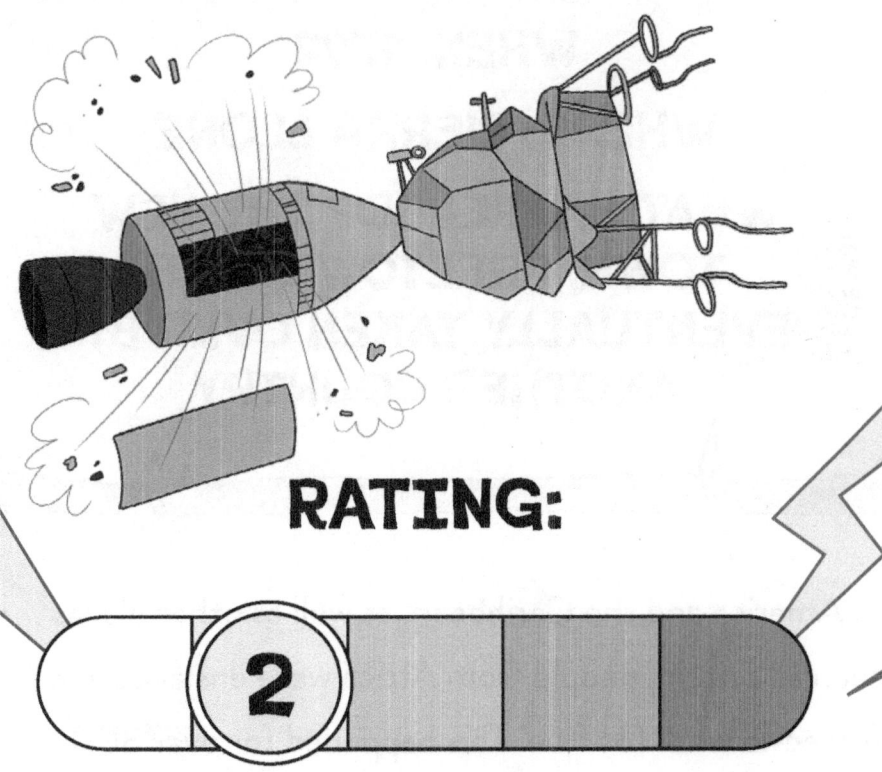

RATING:

2

Because this has a happy ending, it gets a 2. It shows that no matter how dangerous your situation, if you don't panic and think things through, a solution can always be found! Plus, their whole story was made into an EPIC film called *Apollo 13* and, as you've probably noticed, we love a good movie here at Epic Towers!

THE FAIL: PEOPLE DIDN'T MAKE PROPER PLANS WHEN STARTING A NEW TOWN!

WHEN: 1792

WHERE: SIERRA LEONE

WHAT HAPPENED? THE NEW TOWN, FREETOWN, WAS EVENTUALLY TAKEN OVER BY ANOTHER COUNTRY

In America and the Caribbean, as well as other places such as Britain, people from Africa were enslaved and forced to work for free. This happened for over 300 years. In the 1700s, people from across the world began to question why this awful thing was happening and tried to think of ways to make the lives of enslaved people, and people who had managed to escape slavery, better.

A group of people in Britain came up with a plan led by an abolitionist called John Clarkson and an African American man, Thomas Peters. An abolitionist is

someone who campaigned for slavery to be stopped.
At this time, many African Americans had fled to Nova
Scotia in Canada to be free. This led to a new but tiring
life. It was cold, unlike the warm, lush environments they
were used to. Clarkson and Peters thought it would be
a good idea to start a new town in Africa and invited the
former enslaved people in Nova Scotia to go and live
there. Many chose to start a new life in a place that was
eventually called Freetown.

This ambitious plan started to turn into an **EPIC FAIL**
very early on. When the first settlers arrived, it was
mostly jungle and beaches. That
sounds great for a holiday,

AT LEAST WE WON'T
RUN OUT OF WOOD!

but a lot of work for a new life! In the beginning, the settlers were ruled by an English governor who treated them poorly – this was exactly the kind of behaviour they moved to Freetown to avoid! Then, someone forgot to tell the locals, the Temne people, a new town was being established on their turf. The local people didn't feel properly compensated when all these new people just started building on their land. Then, there were rules that meant the new settlers couldn't really mix with the people who were already living in the country. For example, they couldn't spend money anywhere but their own local store.

It was also in a part of the world that was being eyed up by other European colonists. Soon, the town was attacked by the French, the Temne people, and finally the British, who made a colony of what we know as Sierra Leone.

The dream of building a new homeland for former enslaved peoples turned into an **EPIC FAIL** but you can still see evidence of the story today. When Britain took over in 1808, further settlers arrived to join the Nova

Scotians from Jamaica, and all the settlers were given an area of Freetown called Maroon Town, which still exists now. You can still see the presence of these settlers in the culture and language of Sierra Leone today.

RATING:

3

Everyone tried so hard to give people who were once enslaved a better life. Sadly, something as cruel as slavery is never going to have an easy solution. It would have been better to fight for former enslaved peoples to have equal rights in the countries they were born in, than to send them somewhere else.

THE FAIL: THE NAZI PARTY TOLD EVERYONE THAT WHITE EUROPEANS WERE SUPERIOR WHILE HOSTING A SUMMER OLYMPIC GAMES!

WHEN: 1936

WHERE: GERMANY

WHAT HAPPENED? AN AFRICAN AMERICAN WON FOUR GOLD MEDALS AND BECAME WORLD FAMOUS!

In 1936 the Olympics were held in Berlin, when the Nazi party controlled Germany. They were a horrible, racist regime that had horrendous beliefs. The Olympics were meant to be their celebration to show off how strong and powerful they thought they were and prove their belief that 'Aryans' – white people – were the best humans in the world.

Germany won **A LOT** of medals during their home Olympics, but one man stole the show. The Nazi propaganda about which humans they thought were superior was drowned out by the achievements of an American athlete, Jesse Owens.

He won four gold medals, in the long jump, 100m, 200m and in the 4 x 100m relay. This was an incredible achievement and he is now one of America's most famous athletes. Having a Black person as the star of the show really messed up the idea that you could decide who the best humans on the planet were just by looking at them.

The flawed ideas of the Nazi party were revealed by Jesse Owens' dominance and people started to question their really horrible views.

It wasn't just the Nazi party that failed. Other countries thought that if they sent athletes to the games, Germany would eventually turn from fascism and seek closer ties to Europe. If anything, the opposite happened!

At the time, the Nazis thought the Olympics were a great success. The truth is that the face of the 1936 Olympics, almost ninety years after they were held, is still an African American called Jesse Owens, and the Nazi party faced an **EPIC FAIL** trying to convince people otherwise.

RATING:

5

The lies the Nazi party told about different people and their place in society were deeply wrong. We're glad that the legacy of these games is Jesse Owens, and thankfully we know more than ever how horrid the Nazis were.

Real Fail or Fake Fail?

IN 2006 LINDSEY JACOBELLIS FAILED TO WIN AN OLYMPIC GOLD BECAUSE SHE CELEBRATED LEADING THE SNOWBOARD CROSS RACE TOO EARLY AND **SHE FELL!**

Find the answer on page 237.

THE FAIL: ATHENIANS DIDN'T REALISE HOW HARD IT WOULD BE TO TAKE OVER SICILY

WHEN: 415 BCE

WHERE: GREECE

WHAT HAPPENED? AN ANCIENT SUPER-POWER WAS SENT PACKING

In 415 BCE Athens was at the height of its power. Its leaders had won some epic battles and it was a dominant force in the ancient Greek world. Most people would be happy with a situation like that but it's easy to always want more! The leaders of Athens decided they should keep expanding and had their eyes on Sicily, a large island in the Mediterranean Sea. It's the island that Italy looks like it's kicking away! Sicily was run by the Syracusans and the Athenians thought they could easily take it for themselves. They also had some allies on the island. They assumed that their friends would welcome an Athenian takeover . . .

A huge fleet of ships with thousands of soldiers was sent to the island and the Athenians were confident they would win. Unfortunately, they didn't predict that the island would be so well defended. Then, their friends on the island were a bit surprised to see them. Just because you're friends with someone, it doesn't mean you want them come and run your island! You want them to visit and maybe have dinner, not take control of the place.

Finally, someone in Athens might have forgotten to consider they were already fighting a war with Sparta, a state with fighters who became famous for their strength and discipline. As you can imagine, their resources were stretched by both conflicts, and in the end, they didn't have the resources to crush the Syracusan armies.

The fighting continued for around two years and the Athenian army began to run low on supplies. They ended up struggling with a lack of food and equipment and then illness amongst the soldiers.

Finally, in 413 BCE, the Athenian army was surprised by an attack which trapped their ships and completely destroyed them. Their attempt to take over the island ended in defeat. They returned to concentrate on their war with the Spartans, but ended up losing that too. Historians think that this failed power grab marked the beginning of the end of Athenian rule. If that isn't an **EPIC FAIL**, I don't know what is!

RATING:

4

If there is one thing we have learned in this book, it's that empires cannot last forever. However, this still gets a high rating because it was a completely unprovoked war. The Athenians attacked Sicily because they felt like it. And it led to the eventual downfall of an epic Grecian power!

THE FAIL: THE VIKINGS SETTLED IN A FREEZING PART OF THE NORTH AMERICAN CONTINENT

WHEN: 1000 CE

WHERE: VINLAND (IN MODERN-DAY CANADA)

WHAT HAPPENED? THEY PACKED UP AND WENT BACK HOME

Lots of people think Christopher Columbus discovered America but we know better. You can't discover a place if people are already living there. You're visiting with another motive. And Columbus wasn't even the first European to go there.

The Vikings are considered to be the first people to sail to the north American continent from Europe. This should be no surprise because they were extremely skilled sailors and lived on land in the North Atlantic like Greenland and Iceland, so they were already halfway there!

In 1000 CE they landed on the northeastern tip of the continent. In spite of it being as wintery as the place they came from, they found trees that were useful for timber and realised they were able to grow crops too. So they decided to settle. They named their new spot Vinland – probably because it was full of wild grapes and grapes are used to make wine. A whole new country and it's full of grapes? Sounds pretty good, doesn't it?

Not when you get to know all the other stuff the country was full of! The Vikings encountered a few problems while they were there. Indigenous Americans already lived on the land. They were not impressed with their new visitors, especially when the Vikings named their friends 'The Wretched Ones'. That is exactly how you get off on the wrong foot with your new neighbours! The Vikings were also totally outnumbered and it would have been impossible to win any battles against the people whose home they just rocked up to.

This wasn't their only problem. Coming all the way from Europe made it really hard to be sent supplies. It was just too far away to be regularly sent important things like clothes, food and weapons, and they weren't doing a good job at being able to make those things themselves in Vinland either.

Eventually, they had enough and abandoned the distant settlement for good.

RATING:

1

This gets a low score because what the Vikings did made sense. They went somewhere and found people already living on the land, so didn't make themselves at home. And they realised very quickly taking over a whole new continent was more trouble than it was worth!

THE FAIL: A PHARAOH COULDN'T GET HIS SUBJECTS TO WORSHIP THE SUN!

WHEN: 1351 BCE

WHERE: ANCIENT EGYPT

WHAT HAPPENED? HE WAS FORGOTTEN UNTIL HIS TOMB WAS DISCOVERED THOUSANDS OF YEARS LATER

These days, when most leaders start their jobs running an empire or country, they think about the things they are going to do to make things better. Like spend more money on schools and hospitals. If it was me, I would invent the four-day weekend! When Pharaoh Akhenaten came to power in 1351 BCE, he decided he would make all his Egyptian subjects worship Aten the Sun God, as he had decided that this god was the best one. It's not the first thing that comes to mind, is it?

Ancient Egyptians are known for polytheism, which means they worshipped lots and lots of gods. There were thousands of deities. As you can imagine, worshipping only one was a massive change for people to get to grips with.

Akhenaten set to work removing statues and temples that worshipped any god other than Aten the Sun God. He built new monuments which depicted only his all-powerful supreme being.

Despite his efforts, his new religion lasted only about twenty years. People didn't really want to stop worshipping all their other gods, and soon after his changes, a plague swept across northern Egypt. If Aten the Sun God was so great, why did this plague happen?

When Akhenaten died in around 1334 BCE, his son Tutankhamen (yeah, that guy with the supposedly cursed tomb!) decided not only to put things back to how they were, but also to destroy all of the temples and monuments that were built for Aten the Sun God. Eventually, future pharaohs decided to delete Akhenaten's reign from the record, so it would be as if he was never in charge. It wasn't until thousands of years later that archaeologists found evidence of Akhenaten and records of his efforts that his reign was remembered.

He failed to get Egyptians to worship the sun and it's a shame he didn't live in the twenty-first century where it's much easier to find sun worshippers! We love the sun now – remember your hats and sun cream, though!

RATING:

4

Ancient Egypt was a very religious society and it was a bold move to try and change people's beliefs overnight. However, historians are fascinated by Akenhaten's obsession with one god as it is one of the earliest examples of monotheism – when a religion worships a single god. After the end of ancient Egypt, Christianity, Islam and Judaism emerged and those religions all worship a single god. So maybe Akhenaten's legacy is more influential than we think!

Fails for Thought

Everyone in this chapter tried really hard to achieve their goals! But since putting in lots of effort wasn't enough, what other things could they have thought of? Maybe they could have planned better? Or done more research?

CHAPTER EIGHT

EPIC FAILS FROM PEOPLE WHO WERE MEANT TO BE IN CHARGE!

Has a grown-up ever said to you that you have to 'do what you're told!'? They're usually talking about following instructions given to you by someone important, like a teacher or parent. You should do what these people ask you to do, because they tend to know what they are talking about. And they are normally asking you to do something sensible, like 'put your shoes away because people might trip over them!' or 'share your toys!'. But guess what? Important people aren't always right! And when they are wrong, it can sometimes result in an **EPIC FAIL**! I hope you enjoy this chapter about grown-ups with a lot of responsibility who made a mistake. But you should still share your toys and put your shoes away when a grown-up asks, OK?

THE FAIL: RUSSIA SOLD LOTS OF LAND FOR NOT A LOT OF MONEY

WHEN: 1867

WHERE: ALASKA

WHAT HAPPENED? THE AMERICANS FOUND OIL ON THE LAND WHICH IS WORTH A LOT OF MONEY!

We think of Alaska as an American state, but until 1867, it was owned by Russia. If you look for Alaska on a map, this makes complete sense! It's right next to the north-eastern tip of Russa. It's actually not very close to the mainland of America at all. America owns it because one day, Tsar Alexander II, who ruled Russia in the late nineteenth century, decided to sell the icy chunk of land.

Alaska is a beautiful bit of the world. It's full of snow, mountains, forests and wonderful wildlife. However, Russia was already full of snow, mountains and fantastic wildlife. It didn't need more of it! Alaska was an expensive area of land to look after, too. It's on the very edge of the country and its remoteness made it very expensive to defend. It also cost a lot of money to send supplies to the people who lived there.

Russia needed to raise some money just after the Crimean War, so they sold Alaska to the US for $7.2 million in a sale that we now call the Alaska Purchase. At the time, Americans thought they had been ripped off! Over $7 million for ice and bears! People thought this was an **EPIC FAIL** for America.

However, it turned out to be an **EPIC FAIL** for Russia instead. Over time, lots of very expensive things were discovered in Alaska. Oil, gold and even food resources like salmon, which is not cheap!

Not only that, in the decades that followed, America and Russia began to have more and more disagreements. Russia sold all that land to a country that became one of their biggest foes.

Before you sell large chunks of land, it's definitely worth checking if anything valuable is underground beforehand. It's a bit like when I donate clothes to the charity shop – I always check whether or not there is money in the pockets first!

RATING:

3

This gets a 3 because Russia happens to have lots of its own natural resources – so it could just about afford to accidently give some away. However, it is the perfect FAIL for a nation to learn from: make sure you check for oil before you sell your land!

Real Fail or Fake Fail?

THE BLACK DEATH HAPPENED BECAUSE OF CATS!

Find the answer on page 238.

THE FAIL: ANOTHER LEADER MADE GENGHIS KHAN ANGRY

WHEN: 1219

WHERE: MONGOLIA AND MODERN-DAY IRAQ/IRAN

WHAT HAPPENED? HIS COUNTRY WAS INVADED BY GENGHIS KHAN!

Making Genghis Khan angry was not a good idea. Genghis Khan was the ruler of the Mongol Empire and was known for being up for a battle or two. But he was also a clever diplomat and was always looking for opportunities to expand his influence without having to fight in wars. He wasn't quarrelsome all the time!

He wanted to trade with the Khwarazmian Empire and maybe even become allies. This was a huge empire in the 1200s which ruled areas we know today as Uzbekistan, Iran and Turkmenistan. To help build a relationship, Genghis

Khan sent over a few traders to meet the leader of the Khwarazmian Empire, Shah Ala ad-Din Muhammed.

Khan's reputation was well known by Muhammed and he was immediately suspicious. Knowing Khan was always starting wars and taking over land, he saw the visiting traders as a threat. He guessed that the traders were spies, but they really were just sending a message! He ended up killing them, beheading one of them (even though you're not supposed to kill the messenger!) and kidnapping some others.

All of this was an **EPIC FAIL**. Khan quite rightly took this as a sign of hostility and decided to attack the empire and destroyed all their main cities. He was relentless. In less than two years, the whole Khwarazmian empire fell to Khan's armies.

It also started the Mongol takeover of other parts of Asia, which eventually saw them become a dominant force in the region. The next time someone who has a large and well-trained army wants to do business with you, say 'yes!'

RATING:

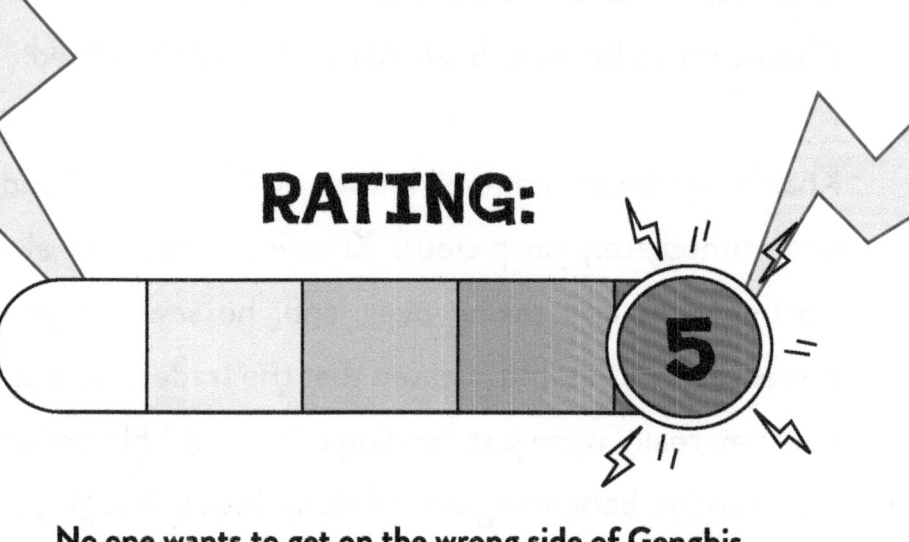

5

No one wants to get on the wrong side of Genghis Khan! Just think, if the two empires had become friends, they could have ruled together, side by side. It's funny that Muhammed thought Genghis Khan was untrustworthy because of his reputation for fighting, when HE'S the one who started the fight in the first place!

Real Fail or Fake Fail?

A MESSENGER TOLD A WHOLE ISLAND THAT A NUCLEAR BOMB WAS COMING!

Find the answer on page 238.

THE FAIL: SOMEONE SAT ON THE WRONG CHAIR!

WHEN: 1900

WHERE: THE GOLD COAST, NOW KNOWN AS GHANA

WHAT HAPPENED? AN EPIC WAR STARTED!

In 1751, Britain established a company to trade with a country they called the Gold Coast on the west coast of Africa. It wasn't a very imaginative name. They just called it that because gold was the main resource they took from the land. They also took diamonds, wood, cocoa and ivory. By 1874, after more than 100 years of controlling the land, they decided to colonise the area and forced the local kingdoms to live under British rule. One of the kingdoms that had to submit to British rule was the Ashanti Empire.

The Ashanti people tried to negotiate with the British because they didn't really want to be ruled by them.

They had a very sacred object called the Golden Stool. It belonged to the king and his people, and it symbolised the unity, power and wealth of the Ashanti Kingdom. It was a bit like a throne or a crown that a European king or queen might own – only people considered special can sit on or wear these things too.

This stool was covered in gold decorations, and it was not allowed to touch the ground. It always had to be placed on a blanket and only the Ashanti king was allowed to touch it. It was not an ordinary stool to the Ashanti people, and the British knew it.

The British governor who was in Ghana at the time, Sir Frederick Hodgson, knew the Golden Stool was sacred. He became obsessed with it. He wanted the Ashanti

people to realise they weren't in control of their land any more – the British were. He had the bright idea of sitting on the stool to make them understand this once and for all.

The Ashantis were shocked. They weren't even allowed to sit on it; it was only for the king, and here came some guy who thought he could sit on it. **EPIC FAIL!** Furious with the placement of his bum, they started a rebellion. They were led by a brave female soldier, the Queen Mother Yaa Asantewaa. Their aim was to remain independent, and protect the stool, of course! They hid the stool, determined that no British person would sit on it again.

The rebellion was initially successful, and Ashanti fighters even manged to storm a fort in Kumasi, where the British had sought refuge. However, it was too difficult to battle the larger and much more advanced British army. After realising how strong the Ashanti fighters were, the British governor asked for more troops and the revolt was ended.

The Ashanti people lost the war in the end but they managed to hide the stool from the British. In fact, they hid it so well even they forgot where it was! No one could find it until it was discovered again in 1920. It was eventually returned to the Ashanti people and you can visit it in Ghana today.

RATING:

4

Sir Frederick Hodgson was determined that the people of the Gold Coast accepted British ownership, but their ability to fight so well in this rebellion was never forgotten. The spirit Hodgson tried to squash by sitting on that stool is the same spirit that made the Gold Coast the first nation in Africa to gain independence in 1957. It gave itself the name Ghana, which means 'warrior king'! That's a much better name, I think!

THE FAIL: A VERY IMPORTANT MEETING WITH VERY IMPORTANT PEOPLE WAS HOSTED IN A ROOM ABOVE A CESSPIT. EURGH!

WHEN: 1184

WHERE: GERMANY

WHAT HAPPENED? LOTS OF PEOPLE FELL INTO LOTS OF POO. GROSS!

Let's get the foul bit out of the way: what is a cesspit? In medieval times, human waste was dealt with in a very unsophisticated way. Vast holes would be dug and all the stinky stuff would be thrown into it. These holes were called cesspits. A cesspit is a pit full of poo. You might want to hold your nose for this **FAIL**!

On 26 July 1184 the king of Germany, Henry VI, called a meeting of very important people in Erfurt, a smallish town in central Germany. There were lots of arguments happening between various nobles at the time, and Henry called a meeting to put a stop to it. The King decided that everyone should meet in the room of a building near the town's cathedral. Everyone who attended was a big deal. Imagine a room containing the King, aristocrats and several counts. It very glamourous, like a medieval Met Gala!

There were many people there – in fact, too many. The creaky wooden floor couldn't take the weight of all the important people and it collapsed, sending all the attendees into the poo pond below. **YUCK**.

Tragically, around sixty people were not able to escape and they drowned in the waste. Henry VI survived because he happened to have been standing in a part of the building made from stone.

Despite the huge toll, the individuals who were called to solve their argument miraculously survived. We do know they ended their argument but the precise nature of the beef has been long forgotten, flushed away into ancient history. If swimming into a pit of poo doesn't put your disagreements with people into perspective, nothing will!

RATING:

5

Of course it's a 5! If you're going organise a meeting full of dignitaries, it's best not to have it above a cesspit. Even if the floor doesn't collapse, imagine the smell!

Fails for Thought

Why do you think some leaders make bad decisions – maybe it's the pressure of being in charge?
What kinds of things would make a leader less likely to fail – is it patience, being bossy, or being a good listener? Can you think of anything else?

CHAPTER NINE

EPIC FAILS THAT WE ARE STILL TRYING TO FIX

The good thing about **EPIC FAILS** is that they often lead to epic solutions. An **EPIC FAIL** can lead to making something safer or easier to use. That's why fails are nothing to be feared! The only problem is, sometimes the epic solution takes a little while to find. It might be a difficult problem to solve, or maybe too expensive. But whatever the issue, it doesn't mean we won't keep trying. Maybe after reading about these fails that we're still trying to fix, you might come up with some ideas!

THE FAIL: A TOWER WAS BUILT ON SOFT LAND

WHEN: 1173

WHERE: PISA

WHAT HAPPENED? IT STARTED TO FALL OVER . . .

The Leaning Tower of Pisa started to lean while it was being built. Now, you'd think if you were building something that wasn't standing up straight, you'd start again, but no, the people building this tower didn't. It all began to go a bit wrong once they'd completed a few floors and they couldn't be bothered to knock it down and start again from the beginning!

Because they wanted the tower to be really amazing, they built it using a very heavy type of stone. This meant they could create its brilliant arches and carve out all its cool columns. However, they didn't check whether the soil they were building it on could hold its heavy weight, which is why one side started to sink into the ground.

The tower took over 200 years to complete, and for hundreds of years after it was finished engineers and architects kept trying to come up with ideas to stop the building from falling.

Finally, about thirty years ago, weights were put inside the tower to stop its lean. It worked so well, they think they might have reversed the lean and people say one day it might become the Standing Straight Tower of Pisa!

RATING:

2

You might think it's a very big fail to make a building that isn't straight, but this building has now become a landmark. It's very clever to build something correctly. But I think it's even cleverer to build something **INCORRECTLY** and still have it standing after hundreds of years!

THE FAIL: THE ROMANS CUT DOWN TOO MANY TREES

WHEN: 476 CE

WHERE: ALL OVER THE ROMAN EMPIRE

WHAT HAPPENED? THE ROMAN EMPIRE BECAME TOO EXPENSIVE TO RUN!

The Roman Empire lasted for around 1,000 years and it was very advanced. Towards its end, it was dealing with a failing economy and invasions from its enemies. And one **EPIC FAIL** did not make things easier: they cut down too many trees.

The Empire needed lots of wood to build ships and buildings, and to burn as fuel. Wood might seem ordinary now but in Roman times it was an incredibly valuable resource and it was common for forests to be cleared to meet the demand for wood. When you cut down lots of trees to use the wood or to use the land for something else, it's called deforestation.

The problem is, trees are really useful when they are left in the ground. If you cut down too many, you have no roots to soak up extra water from rain or overflowing rivers. This leads to flooding and flooding leads to something called soil erosion. This is when soil washes away, taking away all the tasty nutrients. Plants need these nutrients to grow. If you don't have nutritious soil, you can't grow a lot of food! After a while, the Empire wasn't able to grow enough food to feed its people.

Tress do even more! Without trees, lots of land turned to marshland. Insects love marshland, but in the warmer parts of the Empire, they could spread illnesses, such as malaria.

As they cut more and more trees down, the Romans had to find trees that were further and further away from the cities and towns that needed them. This meant it cost more to transport all the wood, making everything more expensive.

The last thing you need while you've got lots of threats on your plate is to run out of a vital resource.

The deforestation was so widespread, the forests never recovered. The Pontine Marshes are marshland in Italy that still exist now because of all the deforestation that happened in Roman times. And the crazy thing is, we're making the same mistakes with our forests today.

RATING:

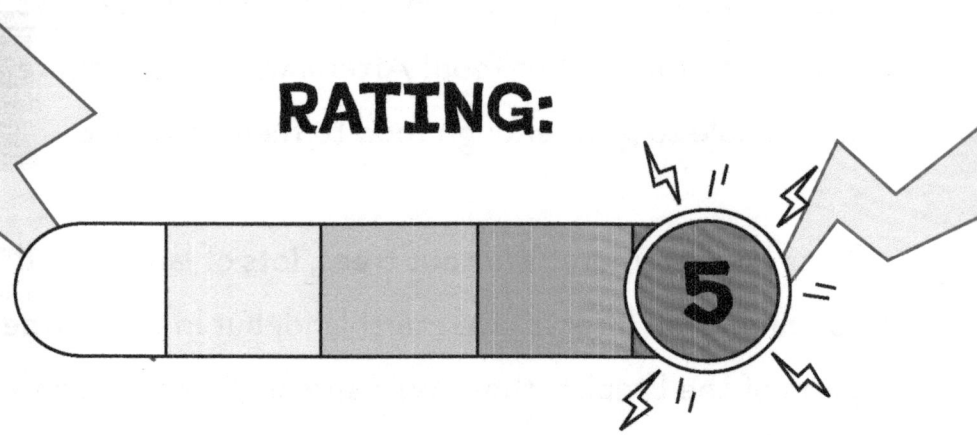

5

The Romans cleared huge areas of forest and woodland that remain bare. We often come across empires that fall because they can't protect their land from their enemies. We also need to learn about empires that can't protect their land from themselves! The sad thing is, deforestation is something that is still happening around the world and we are still yet to learn the lesson of the Romans and their **EPIC DEFORESTATION FAIL!**

THE FAIL: A REALLY ANNOYING WEED WAS BROUGHT TO THE UK

WHEN: 1850

WHERE: ALL OVER BRITAIN

WHAT HAPPENED? WE HAVE A PLANT THAT CAN TAKE DOWN BUILDINGS!

Japanese knotweed is a plant that was brought to the UK by a doctor called Philipp Franz von Siebold. He was on a volcano in Japan (which wouldn't be my top holiday destination!) and found what he thought was a very pretty plant.

He sent samples to Kew Gardens, a famous place in London that stores plant seeds for research, as well as growing and selling them. They thought it was very pretty too and cultivated and sold the plant to households.

Unfortunately, once Japanese knotweed starts growing, it's impossible to stop. Its roots grow thickly and deeply into the ground and can destroy the foundations of buildings. It's almost impossible to get rid of and can only be properly destroyed – if you do manage to pull it from the ground – by burning it. It's like some kind of zombie plant!

It seems bringing a plant back from a volcano and thinking it would make a good garden plant is an **EPIC FAIL!**

There is nothing we can do about Japanese knotweed now. We have to live with it and try to destroy it when we find it. When it's found, experts have to dig it out, then burn what they find to make sure it can't grow again. Next time you're on holiday on a volcano, leave the plants alone. Bring back a fridge magnet instead.

RATING:

People used to bring all kinds of plants back from their travels in the nineteenth century as the world was still a new and interesting place that only a few privileged people got to see any of. It was considered generous to bring back samples from glamourous and far-flung places. However, looks can be deceiving. Perhaps the best thing to do if you see an attractive plant that you haven't seen before is to STUDY IT before you take it to a different country!

THE FAIL: RABBITS WERE TAKEN TO AUSTRALIA

WHEN: 1859

WHERE: AUSTRALIA

WHAT HAPPENED? AUSTRALIA HAS A LOT OF RABBITS NOW!

Do you ever get bored when you go away? British people who went to Australia in the nineteenth century had exactly this problem. One of their favourite hobbies was going out to the countryside and hunt rabbits. But there were no rabbits in Australia!

Thomas Austin was an English settler in Australia who decided he'd had enough of being bored. He managed to get some rabbits sent to him and he let thirteen of them out on to his estate so he and his friends could go out and hunt them. *Scrabble* wasn't invented until 1948, so I guess they had to think of something to do!

Releasing those rabbits turned into an **EPIC FAIL**. Just seven years later, those thirteen rabbits had grown to over 14,000.

The rabbits quickly spread beyond Thomas Austin's estate. In 1880 they had gone into New South Wales. By 1886, they reached Queensland and by 1894 they had taken over all of Australia. Rabbits spread across Australia more quickly than any other introduced species in the world.

This might not seem like a bad thing because they are very, very cute, but this was an **EPIC FAIL** because rabbits are an **INVASIVE** species, just like Japanese knotweed. They spread quickly, eat crops and don't have many natural predators that can control their numbers. By the 1940s there were 600 million rabbits in Australia.

Australians tried to build rabbit-proof fences, including a very famous one that was over 3,000 km long. It was a bit like the Great Wall of China, but for little furry animals. It didn't work, though, because rabbits were often already on the other side of the fence, and they could burrow underneath it, or sneak through holes. Walls were more effective against the Mongols than they were against rabbits!

RATING:

4

Invasive species ruin ecosystems. It's pretty selfish to import animals for your own hobbies and change the environment completely. I wonder if it was worth it? I bet Thomas Austin had so many rabbits to shoot he probably got bored and started a new hobby.

CHAPTER TEN

OOOPS, THEY DID IT AGAIN!

EPIC FAILS are often very handy because they can stop us making the same mistakes in the future. Well – they are supposed to! Sometimes we make the same mistakes again when we think we failed in the past because of bad luck. Sometimes the **EPIC FAIL** was such a long time ago that we forget about it and do it again. And sometimes it's because some grown-ups never learn! Let's all scratch our heads at some mistakes people made when they should have known better. What were they thinking?

THE FAIL: PEOPLE KEPT SETTING FIRE TO THE LIBRARY OF ALEXANDRIA

WHEN: 48 BCE, 391 CE, 641 CE

WHERE: EGYPT

WHAT HAPPENED? I TOLD YOU! PEOPLE KEPT SETTING FIRE TO THE LIBRARY!

Do you remember Julius Caesar accidently burning down the Library of Alexandria in 48 BCE? Well, he wasn't the only one!

After it burned down the first time, the library was rebuilt by the Romans. However, it still had to be defended. In the third century CE, Emperor Aurelian fought lots of battles to help keep control of Alexandria, but once again, the library was destroyed in one of his epic battles.

Bishop Theodosius, who ran Alexandria between 385 CE and 412 CE, ordered the library to be destroyed and replaced with a church in 391 CE. During this time, people thought religion was more important than things like history and science. They didn't mind when the library's collections were ordered to be destroyed as they had decided that the knowledge in this library was blasphemous.

Finally, in 641 CE, the region was ruled by a leader called Caliph Umar, who had the same beliefs. It's said he ordered all the remaining scrolls in the library to be destroyed and used to heat the city's bath houses. Can you imagine burning a book just so you could have a hot bath? I would prefer a cold shower to burning a book!

RATING:

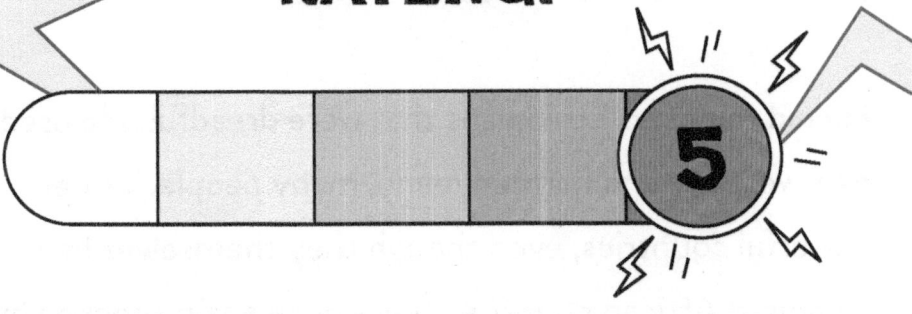

5

Today, we can't imagine burning a library. We are much better at understanding that faith and knowledge can live very happily alongside each other. Still, there is so much we don't know about the ancient world, because all the goodies in this ancient library were lost.

THE FAIL: ITALY TRIED TO COLONISE ETHIOPIA AGAIN!

WHEN: 1935

WHERE: ETHIOPIA

WHAT HAPPENED? ITALY WAS LEFT EMPTY HANDED, AGAIN!

Remember Italy epically failing to take over Ethiopia? In 1935 a new leader was in charge called Mussolini. He decided that it was time to try and take over Ethiopia again. After the **EPIC FAIL** of the past, he thought the way to get the country was to be even more awful and brutal the second time round.

He did things to Ethiopians that were dreadful. He used new weapons and harmed many, many people. Other powerful countries, even though they themselves had colonised African countries, were once again shocked by his methods.

The Italians came across the same problems as last time.

Ethiopians were good at resisting the Italian armies and, as before, they got a lot of support. And this time around, support came from outside the continent too!

It's an amazing story. African Americans heard about the struggle and were inspired to help. They trained to join the military and even sent money and supplies. A people's march for Ethiopia in Harlem drew 25,000 African Americans and anti-fascist Italian Americans who hated what they were witnessing. In 1941, with help from America and all their other allies, Ethiopia defeated the Italian army.

In 1942, Ethiopia was recognised as an independent country. Again!

RATING:

5

They did it again! They completely underestimated the Ethiopian fighters, and without help from other European countries, tried to do it alone. Italy's EPIC FAIL was a mission that was doomed to fail.

THE FAIL: TOADS WERE TAKEN TO AUSTRALIA

WHEN: 1935

WHERE: AUSTRALIA

WHAT HAPPENED? AUSTRALIA NOW HAS A LOT OF TOADS!

Remember the rabbits taking over Australia? It was the turn of the toads next.

Toads sound just as sweet as rabbits, but they are not that cute if you're an indigenous Australian plant or animal species. This particular species, the cane toad, is usually found in North and South America – nowhere near Australia! But it was introduced in 1935 as it was thought it could help protect valuable sugar crops.

When settlers went to Australia, one of the things they did was grow sugar cane and make sugar to sell. There was one thing in their way – Australian beetles who loved to eat sugar cane.

When someone discovered that the cane toad ate beetles, they released them into the sugar cane fields. If they ate the beetles, there would be no pesky pest to eat their sugar cane! However, instead of eating the beetles, the toads ate everything else!

This was a disaster. Now, as well as the beetles, they had another pest that was eating all their other crops. And because the cane toad was an invasive species, it had no predators to control their numbers. And, if other animals tried to eat the cane toad, they would die, because it has poisonous skin!

This damaged wildlife even further.

WHAT'S WRONG, TOAD? YOU HAVEN'T TOUCHED YOUR BEETLES!

Birds and reptiles often ate the toads by mistake because they look a bit like frogs. So, this **FAIL** ended up killing wildlife by accident, too!

The cane toad is now considered a pest in Australia. People thought they were doing the right thing by introducing it, but it was an **EPIC FAIL** to not think about how the toad would impact existing wildlife and the environment.

RATING:

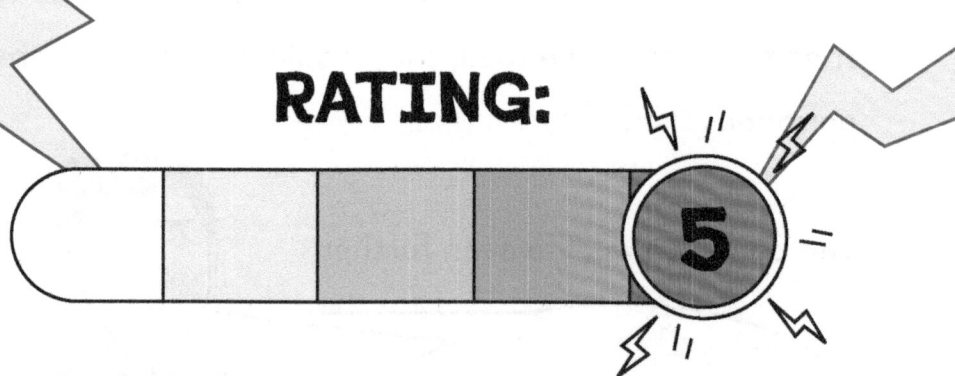

5

A toad-ally disastrous fail! Today, it's very hard to take toads, or any animals, to Australia. They did learn about the dangers of bringing in new wildlife, but they learned a little too late!

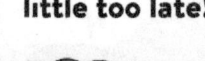

THE FAIL: GERMANY INVADED RUSSIA WHEN IT WAS COLD

WHEN: 1941

WHERE: RUSSIA

WHAT HAPPENED? HITLER FAILED AND EVENTUALLY LOST THE WAR

In 1941, the Second World War was going quite well for Germany, and Hitler felt confident that he could take over Russia. He was obsessed with the German domination of Europe and for this, control of Russia was essential. It had resources like oil, and a huge population that could give Germany exactly the power it craved. This invasion was called Operation Barbarossa.

Hitler was so determined that he sent over 3 million German soldiers, thousands of tanks and planes to attack the Soviet Union. This caught Russia by surprise. Unfortunately for the German army, things caught them by surprise too, which really wouldn't have happened if they had done their homework and studied the **EPIC FAILS** of the past!

The German soldiers were not ready for the extreme cold and snow. They didn't have warm clothes or enough supplies. Their tanks and machinery couldn't work in the ultra-cold temperatures either.

Russia may have been surprised, but they were better trained for the conditions, and better equipped. Soon, they were able to push the advancing German army back. However, they did this slowly and both sides suffered huge, devastating losses.

Germany's plan failed and Russia managed to resist the invasion. It proved to be one of the biggest **EPIC FAILS** during the Second World War. The German losses weakened its army and made it easier for the Allies to fight and eventually win the war.

RATING:

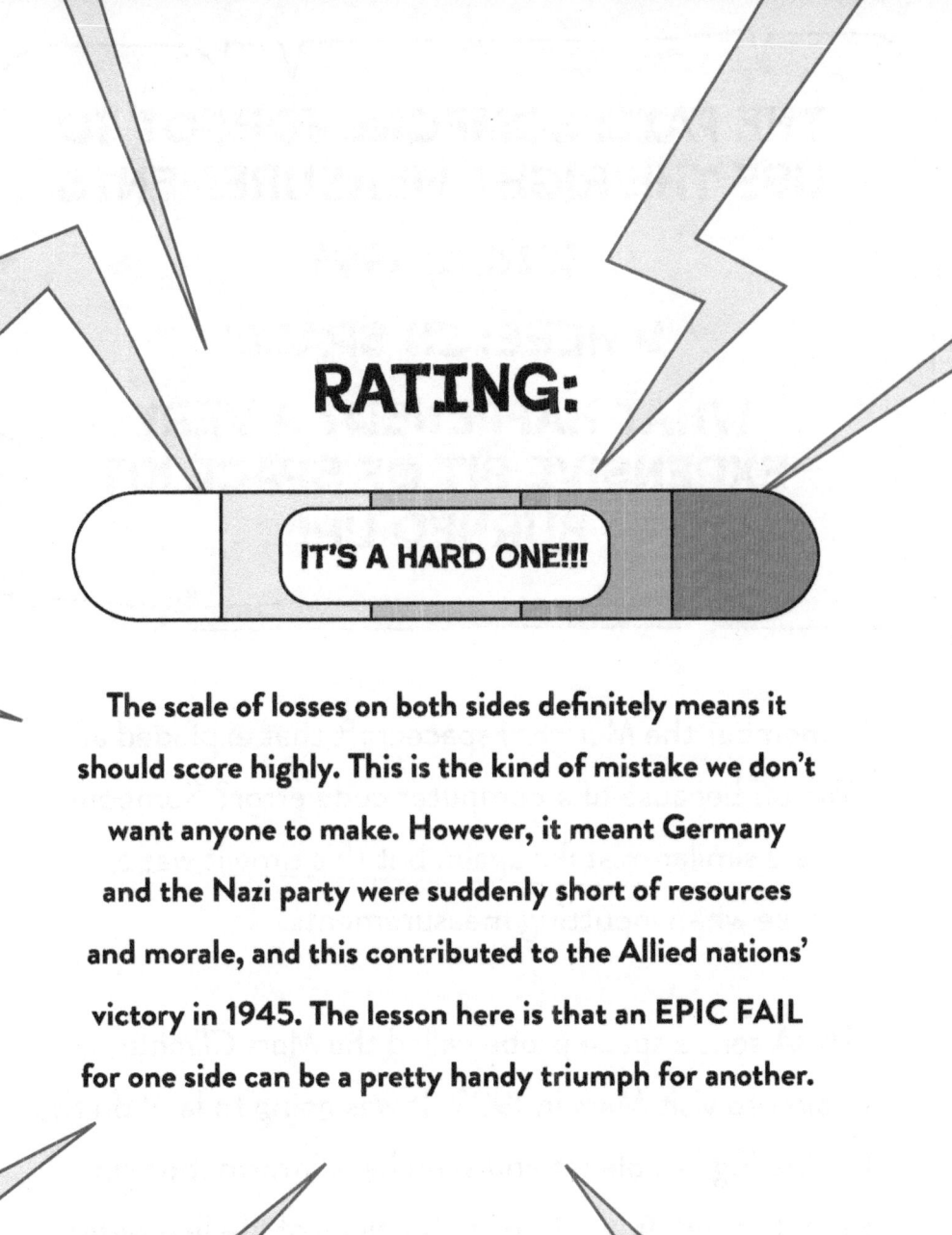

IT'S A HARD ONE!!!

The scale of losses on both sides definitely means it should score highly. This is the kind of mistake we don't want anyone to make. However, it meant Germany and the Nazi party were suddenly short of resources and morale, and this contributed to the Allied nations' victory in 1945. The lesson here is that an EPIC FAIL for one side can be a pretty handy triumph for another.

THE FAIL: SOMEONE FORGOT TO
USE THE RIGHT MEASUREMENTS

WHEN: 1999

WHERE: IN SPACE!

WHAT HAPPENED? A VERY
EXPENSIVE BIT OF SPACE KIT
BURNED UP!

Remember the *Mariner 1* spacecraft that exploded after take-off because of a computer code error? Someone made a similar mistake again, but this time it was a mistake when inputting measurements.

NASA sent a space probe called the *Mars Climate Orbiter* to visit Mars in 1999. It was going to land on the fascinating red planet and send back information on what it found. It was looking for signs of life like water or aliens, and would send back information about the planet's atmosphere and weather conditions.

Sadly, it never made it to the surface of Mars. It burned up in the Martian atmosphere. People couldn't believe it.

The Orbiter had travelled for ten months. It was almost there! How could it be so close, yet so far?

Unfortunately, people had made an **EPIC FAIL** much earlier in the mission, and no one realised. The navigation team that was telling the spacecraft where to go used the **METRIC SYSTEM** of millimetres and meters in its calculations. The team that built the spacecraft used the **IMPERIAL SYSTEM** of inches and feet. This meant the instructions the spacecraft was trying to follow when it needed to land were all wrong and didn't make sense. When it was time to land on Mars, the $125 million craft was sent plummeting into the atmosphere far too quickly, and it burned on entry. With such a big **FAIL** lurking in its systems, I think it's a miracle it got so close to Mars in the first place!

RATING:

3

Obviously NASA had to learn after that epic fail! They standardised units across all projects and teams to make sure everyone was using the same measurements.

Real Fail or Fake Fail?

AN ANCIENT AND POWERFUL SAMURAI ARMY LOST A BATTLE .... BECAUSE THEY WERE TOO BUSY CELEBRATING TO REALISE THEY WERE UNDER ATTACK!

Find the answer on page 238.

THE FAIL: NARWHALS WERE CONSTANTLY MIXED UP WITH UNICORNS

WHEN: FOR AGES! NARWHALS HAVE BEEN TRICKING US ALL FOR THOUSANDS OF YEARS

WHERE: ALL OVER THE WORLD

WHAT HAPPENED? NARWHALS KEPT LOSING THE TITLE OF 'BEST HORNED ANIMAL' TO AN ANIMAL THAT DOESN'T EVEN EXIST!

Unicorns are mythological creatures that appear in stories from all over the world. Some of these stories are over 2,000 years old! You can find unicorns in Greek, Celtic, Viking, Babylonian, Chinese and Indus cultures (in what is now northern India and Pakistan). For some reason, despite never actually seeing one, many of these societies **FAILED** to realise the famous horned horse never actually existed!

Waaaaay back in 1551, a Swiss scientist called Konrad Gesner decided he would write a book that contained a description of all the animals that lived on Earth. Some people think that he got his information from travellers, so animals were included in his book that he hadn't seen himself, including the majestic unicorn. That's not a very good way to do your research, Konrad! **EPIC FAIL!**

Unicorn horns were desired by rich and powerful people looking for good luck charms and cures. Science wasn't always based on facts in those days and people believed unicorn horns could cure a range of illnesses, from epilepsy to the plague.

This gave people a good reason to find things that look a bit like unicorn horns, sell them to the rich folk and makes themselves some cash. Enter – the narwhal. Narwhals are a species of whale that live in the North Atlantic. They are very special animals because they have what horses do not – a long tusk growing out of their head, which looks a bit like a unicorn's horn. For centuries their tusks were sold to people who believed in their powers and wanted their own unicorn horn.

In 1533, Pope Clement VII gave King Francis I of France a 'unicorn' horn that was displayed in a solid gold case. King Philip II of Spain was rumoured to have twelve of them – we are not sure what for, though! Queen Elizabeth I was rumoured to have owned a tusk worth about as much as the price of one of her castles. She believed drinking from a cup made of a unicorn horn would cure a person if they had been poisoned.

It's amazing to think how easily tricked they were. If I was a posh person with a lot of money, I would personally ask for my unicorn horn to be attached to the rest of the unicorn, but then I do drive a hard bargain.

Eventually, science and chemistry progressed. People realised that unicorns did not exist and that animal bits don't have magical properties. However, after centuries of these beliefs, unicorns have cemented themselves well into our imaginations. They are an epic pretend animal and even we at Epic History Towers do love to indulge in a unicorn story every now and then!

RATING:

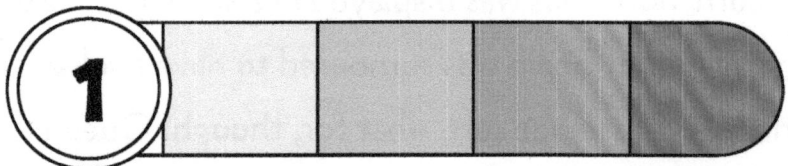

It was a bit crackers to think that a unicorn horn could cure illnesses, but back then people didn't know as much about science and medicine as we do now. They believed in lots of things we now think of as very ridiculous. And unicorns still might exist – we just haven't found one yet!

THE FINAL FAIL

We've done it! We've failed our way through history and we have visited some incredibly **EPIC FAILS**. There were so many to get through and we've only scratched the surface.

After finishing this book, I think we can all agree on the following lessons:

- An **EPIC FAIL** can happen to anyone.
- **FAILING** is part of any process – the trick is to learn from your fails!
- Don't give up!
- Don't panic! Sometimes a **FAIL** can help you discover something new.

And, when we come across a fail we definitely don't want to happen again, we can study what went wrong to make sure the same mistake isn't made twice.

HOORAY FOR FAILS!

GLOSSARY

Here you will find explanations for some of the tougher or more unusual words you might have come across in this book.

AIRSHIP – a type of aircraft made up of a rigid balloon filled with gas which is lighter than air, enabling it to fly

ANTIBIOTIC – a type of medicine that is used to prevent or treat infections caused by bacteria

CATASTROPHE – an event that happens suddenly, causing lots of damage and destruction

COMPANY – a type of business that aims to make money by providing goods or services

COLONISATION - the process of settling and taking control, often forcibly, over the Indigenous people of an area or country

COMPUTER CODE – the instructions, written in special programming languages, that allow computers to perform certain tasks

DYNASTY – a line of rulers, from the same family, who are in charge of a country over many generations – e.g. the Normans in England or the Shang dynasty in ancient China

EMPIRE – a group of countries that are ruled over by a single ruler or state – e.g. the British Empire or the Roman Empire

EXPERIMENT – a scientific test undertaken to try to make a discovery or prove a hypothesis

EXPEDITION – a journey taken by a group of people, for the purpose of exploration, discovery or research

FORTIFICATIONS – a defensive line, made up of walls, towers, moats, etc., used to keep out an invading force

HYPOTHESIS – an idea or concept you test with an experiment

INVASION – when one country tries to take over another using force

INVASIVE – something that spreads quickly through an ecosystem, often a plant or animal

INVENTION – the act of coming up with something new, particularly a device

LABORATORY – a room made for conducting scientific experiments

METRIC SYSTEM – a system of measurement that includes centimetres, metres, litres and grams

PILGRIMAGE – a journey to a special holy place

PHYSICS – the area of science concerned with nature, light, sound, electricity, magnetism and more

SETTLER – a person who moves with a group to live in a new country or place, sometimes displacing those who are already there

TRADE – buying or selling goods, often across countries

REAL OR FAKE ANSWERS

PAGE 22

REAL FAIL! The original Moon landing tapes were deleted so the tapes could be re-used. That was one giant mistake! Luckily, copies had to be made so the Moon landings could be broadcast on TV. American broadcaster CBS saved the day by returning a copy they used for their broadcast to NASA. Phew.

PAGE 45

REAL FAIL! Isambard Kingdom Brunel, hot off the success of all his other cool buildings like the Clifton Suspension Bridge and the Great Western Railway decided to design and build a ship called the *Great Eastern* that could sail between Britain and America. The project was a big FAIL and lost lots of money! Eventually, the vessel was converted into a cable-laying ship, used to lay cables under the Atlantic Ocean. These were used for phone lines – so we can speak to people on the other side of the world. WOO! Brunel was a such a genius that even his failures resulted in really useful things!

PAGE 56

FAKE FAIL! He actually said, 'If you are afraid of failing, you won't get very far' and he was right!

PAGE 70

FAKE FAIL! King Pyrrhus of Epirus did lose a battle in 272 BCE when an old woman threw something at him, but it was a roof tile! It knocked him out and allowed an enemy soldier to attack and kill him.

PAGE 106

REAL FAIL! It is said that at the funeral, his pet parrot had to be removed because it was saying lots of naughty words. I think he had a FOWL mouth, hahaha!

PAGE 171

REAL FAIL! It's not the end of the story, though, as she went on to win gold, finally, sixteen years later!

PAGE 187

FAKE FAIL! The Black Death was spread by rats. Sadly, people thought that it was spread by cats, so lots of them were killed, even though that led to the disease spreading further, because they weren't around to kill the rats.

PAGE 191

REAL FAIL! In 2018 an employee at the Hawai'i Emergency Management Agency mistook a drill for a real nuclear attack on the island. He pressed a button to let everyone know and for thirty-eight minutes people in Hawai'i thought they were about to be hit by a nuclear bomb. OOOPS!

PAGE 228

REAL FAIL! Imagawa Yoshimoto was a Japanese feudal lord who lost the Battle of Okehazama in 1560, partly because his army was partying too much, celebrating previous victories.

Photo Natasha Pszenicki; © Athena Kugblenu

Athena Kugblenu is a stand-up comedian and writer.
She has written for CBBC's *Horrible Histories* series,
CBBC's *Odd Squad*, CBeebies' *JoJo and Gran Gran*,
among many other amazing shows. She is the co-host
of *Bust or Trust?*, a podcast for curious kids. *History's Most
Epic Fibs* and *History's Most Epic Fails* are her first
books for children.

FIND THE FIRST BOOK
IN THE SERIES . . .